OVER THE MOUNTAINS TO
CHENA HOT SPRINGS

A Coming-of-Age Memoir of
a Girl's Family Life in Rural Alaska

GWEN WILSON EILERS

Editorial assistance by Chuck Gray and
daughter-in-law Jeanne Kim Gray

PUBLICATION
CONSULTANTS
We Believe In The Power Of Authors

PO Box 221974 Anchorage, Alaska 99522-1974
books@publicationconsultants.com, www.publicationconsultants.com

ISBN Number: 978-1-59433-897-7
eBook ISBN Number: 978-1-59433-898-4
ISBN Numbers, Library of Congress Number,
Publication Dates, Publishers Information

Manufactured in the United States of America

**One of the four original cabins still standing
when the Wilsons arrived in 1954.**

ABOUT THE AUTHOR

Gwen Wilson Eilers, an elderly retired music teacher, tells the story of her Alaskan family buying and refurbishing the abandoned Chena Hot Springs Resort in the mid-1950's. True to the pioneering spirit inherited from her ancestors who migrated west in the 18th and 19th centuries, Gwen's family of five (two younger brothers) partially lived off the land, facing physical and emotional hardships with resourceful energy.

While Gwen was researching the Springs she became facinated with another Wilson, George W. Wilson (no relation), the "Canadian" who first saw commercial value in the springs and homesteaded the area in 1908, starting his ten-year legal battle for ownership. Gwen successfully intertwines the lives of both Wilsons in her book.

Gwen finished two years of grade school by correspondence at the Springs, then boarded in Fairbanks for four years of high school, still helping the family during the summer months. Her college years were much the same with summers spent at Chena Hot Springs.

Gwen began writing her story as diary entries and short stories at age 12 and continued occasionally writing throughout her life—schooling, marriage, child-rearing and the death of her husband. She recently wrote the last chapters to bring this book to press. Gwen currently resides in Iowa, on her late husband's family farm—the one with an apple tree growing up inside the old windmill.

CONTENTS

Author appreciates assistance from
Steve Gray, Cover design
Dee Dee Hammond, Route Map
Ray Bonnell, Cabin Sketch

———————————

Photos from the Wilson family collection, Chuck Gray and others as
credited.

Prologue

Thousands journeyed to Alaska in the 20th century, pursuing their dreams. This is a story about discovery, the challenges of frontier life, and a 12-year-old girl who believed in her father's dream.

Spanning seventy years, based on factual accounts of two unrelated men with the same last name, this story follows the pursuit and conflict of dreams in an untamed civilization founded by the discovery of gold, and the subsequent obsession with a mineral hot springs in the Tanana Valley of Interior Alaska.

In 1908, George W. Wilson, a Canadian citizen, filed for homesteading rights to 320 acres on Monument Creek, a tributary of the North Fork of the Big Chena River, 60 miles northeast of Fairbanks, Alaska. Thanks to the 1890s discovery of gold in the north country, Big Chena Hot Springs became a popular, though rustic, winter retreat for miners.

By 1913, the United States government had filed suit against Wilson, contesting his right of ownership to the prized retreat, believed to possess "a curative quality second to none in the United States." Given the Springs' unique utility for treating everything from rheumatism to blood disorders, locals felt the land should be kept in American ownership, if such a natural resource could be claimed at all. Years of legal proceedings ensued, but in the end George Wilson prevailed in his homestead claim. He then leased the operation to Charles and Mrs. Beam of Fairbanks, who managed the Chena Hot Springs resort from August, 1911.

Over four decades later, Carl E. Wilson, his wife Edithbelle and their three children embark on an unusual journey. Leaving Fairbanks with a D4 Caterpillar, an army jeep and trailer, a swamp buggy, two kittens and a dog named Totem, the family crosses the rugged mountains of the Alaskan Interior to reach the deserted Hot Springs. In the years that follow, this enterprising family not only establishes a business, but also manages to raise a close-knit family, as they face the rigors of frontier life with grit and humor.

CHAPTER 1

Discovery

"My brother had the rheumatism and there was one fellow told me,
'Why didn't I take him up to the hot springs that were on the Chena.'"
– Thomas Swan

Summer, 1905

Their eyes were fixed on only the river now, watching for jagged logs beneath the ripples of a current, now calmer. They would see challenge enough without having to mend a damaged boat in the middle of nowhere.

Leaving the ice-scarred riverfront of Fairbanks behind, the long, narrow poling boat headed northeast into a glaring sun, up the murky, gray waters of the Big Chena River. Ahead, the hills of the uninhabited interior of Alaska looked peaceful, a new spring quietly waiting to burst forth.

The unexplored waters reflected silver as the two men studied the river through squinted eyes. They weren't sure what lay ahead as they poled beyond the flats and into the hills northeast of town, but a surge of certainty told Thomas Swan that he and his brother, Robert, were onto something big. Thomas Swan was sixteen years younger than his brother Robert. The Swans had arrived in Fairbanks from Pennsylvania a year earlier. The brothers were curious and enduring like their immigrant Scottish father, hoping to find gold in the soils

of the Tanana Valley. Now, however, Robert had rheumatism so bad
he could barely use his right arm.

Thomas had planned to take Robert to the Manley Hot Springs in
the Lower Tanana country, till a co-worker from Fairbanks suggested
taking Robert to the hot springs up the Chena River northeast of
town. The year before, a United States Geological Survey crew
worked between Fairbanks and Circle. Although reports had never
been confirmed, word was out that the crew saw steam rising from
the hills not far from the headwaters of the Chena River.

**Every year the Chena River overflowed its banks during breakup, but
the spring of 1905 was particularly bad for high water and bank erosion.**
*(Courtesy Reed Family papers. Alaska and Polar Regions collection, Rasmusen
Library, UAF.)*

The location was vague. The Swans, unfamiliar with the course
of the Chena River, had no idea what break-up might have done to
the river east of town. Earlier that spring, the ground rumbled in
Fairbanks as river ice ruptured into huge chunks, hurled onto the
riverbanks. Men, women, and children scattered from the riverfront
as giant slabs thundered into the pilings of the wooden bridge spanning the Chena River. The bridge broke like matchsticks and swept
downstream as ice punched out the wooden sidewalk that wound
along First Avenue. Walls of water and tons of ice crashed into the
log cabin businesses facing the river. The settlers watched in horror,

helpless, as the most violent spring break-up they had ever witnessed tore their town apart.

As warmer days melted the ice and the run-off waters receded to the banks of the Chena River, the residents began to put their town back together, but the damage was not over. An unusually heavy snowfall that winter left snowdrifts thawing in the hills above town, flowing down through the birch and spruce timber to the creeks and streams which emptied into the already bulging Chena River. Soon the waters oozed into town again, this time as far as Sixth Avenue, seeping under shop doors and into log cabin homes, sullying so many charming living rooms and cozy kitchens. Residents carried their personal belongings outside to dry out. They postponed the seeding of sustenance vegetable gardens. Forced to face the elemental fury of the land they had chosen, the settlers again rallied to save the town.

The unruly interior of Alaska was a bewitching place. Wide, flat river valleys wove through vast mountain ranges. Dense woods (the men saw lumber for new construction) shrouded plentiful game. Freshwater streams glistened with grayling. Fairbanks was only four years old, yet already the city bustled with nearly 5,000 residents, many of whom were drawn to the region by gold, or the appeal of frontier living.

James Wickersham and his wife had moved from Illinois to Tacoma in Washington Territory, where he served as country probate judge. In 1898, he was elected to the Washington Territory House of Representatives. In 1900, President William McKinley appointed the politically powerful Wickersham as the first judge to sit for Interior Alaska.

By 1901, Federal Judge Wickersham had just cleaned up the court system in Nome, but that was only the beginning of his influence in shaping the future of Alaska. While still stationed at Eagle on the Upper Yukon, the enterprising judge considered the potential of the booming Fairbanks settlement. He envisioned the Tanana Valley as a future farming community. In 1903, he hauled the court records on a dogsled from Eagle to Fairbanks. The townspeople applauded

Wickersham for setting the cornerstone for the frontier town's future growth.

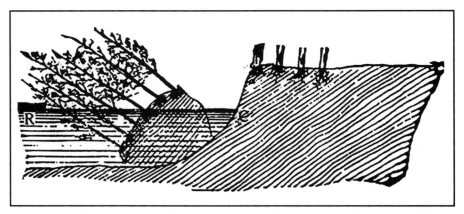

From Lt. Allen's 1885 exploration of Alaska rivers, a depiction of how sweepers are formed along the cut banks of rivers.

On his way back to Eagle, the judge met a merchant, Captain E. T. Barnett, who was stranded at Unakleet on his way to the Tanana River with trading supplies for the Indians and prospectors there. Captain Barnette eventually built a small log cabin on the banks of the Chena River and began to service a handful of prospectors who boasted of yellow sprinkles in the gravel of the Tanana Valley. The next summer, seventeen miles from Barnette's one-room trading post, a major gold strike was hit. Wickersham and Barnett were destined to meet again.

On foot, by water, in groups or alone, prospectors arrived in droves with visions of finding wealth laying in the Tanana Valley streams. These stampeders had missed finding their fortunes in Dawson and Nome in the late 1890s Klondike Gold Rush. Here, they thought the gold dust would be quick to pan and fill their pokes. Instead, they found frozen muskeg and thick layers of dirt and rock, sometimes a hundred feet below the surface before they could even get at the gold on bedrock. For most, the interior of Alaska was an altogether frozen land. Those with a "get rich quick" disposition left quickly for easier diggings; the tough ones stayed and built a town.

Summer days were warm, with daylight all night. The pioneers cut unpeeled spruce logs, scraped up sawdust from the ground to insulate their cabin walls, and edged the streets with wooden sidewalks. The new town was not a typical pioneer settlement, for the people who built it had their mettle tested by a fierce climate. The astute Judge Wickersham promised to do everything in his power to help Captain Barnette succeed, if Barnette would name his trading post Fairbanks, after his fellow Republican, Charles W. Fairbanks, a powerful Senator from Indiana.

The first winter turned bitter cold. There was little food stock and less daylight in the desolate land. In the dark months, settlers took long journeys by dogsled over ice-covered waterways in search of game animals. Fairbanks grew, and each succeeding spring, when the warm rays of the sun returned, miners, prospectors and town residents met on the banks of the Chena River to watch nature's ice show and to celebrate that they had survived one more vicious winter.

The Swan brothers were loaded with enough food and gear to last several weeks. They made their way to the headwaters of the Big Chena River, noting that signs of destruction from the spring break-up grew more severe as they wound between the rolling hills above the flat Tanana Valley. The brothers soon realized they were in for a tough trip. Under normal river conditions and with long poles, the Swans could easily push a heavily-loaded poling boat upstream ten miles a day. But here, birch and spruce trees bent over or lay broken, half out of the river. Gravel bars were covered with silt and stumps, and on river bends where waters had savagely cut away the banks, sweepers resembled porcupines, with quills jutting out of the water.

Their poling boat had a flat bottom of sawed lumber and a narrow stern, a common design for navigating the rivers of Interior Alaska. The man poling in the stern of the boat could switch sides easily. They poled by staying on the shallow or bar side of the river where the current was slower and the water shallow. Robert, nearly sixty years old, was not a strong man, and his arthritis ached. Would they have to turn back? Could they find a way up the river when the current grew faster and deeper?

If there was a hot springs near enough to Fairbanks and the mining camps, Robert and the other men could soak their aching bodies, relieving the pain they suffered from unhealthy diets and hours of hard labor. All winter the prospectors dug deep into the icy earth with only the dim glow from a fire to thaw the frozen ground. By day, in the winter's frigid blackness, they shoveled heaps of thawed earth in grimy, ash-covered boots and wet clothing, pulled buckets of rock, muck and ashes to the top of the shaft and dumped it into large piles, or tailings. With each shovelful they prayed to see glimmers of gold. When spring came, the temperatures warmed and the creeks ran, the prospectors shoveled the mounds of gravel into wooden sluice boxes for washing. The weary men cheered when they eventually spotted gold at the bottom of the sluices. Across the valley floor of Interior Alaska the worthless gravel and muck dredged from the rivers left a map of tailings to chart their story. What is not obvious is that many of the miners developed rheumatism and stomach ailments from so many hours of grueling work in the glacial rivers.

The brothers had heard rumors of steaming hot, medicinal waters with unique healing powers that could cure cripples. The tales swirled like minnows—folks so badly inflicted they could hardly walk, until they soaked themselves in the wondrous waters. Some soaked their pain nearly away, others walked again and some, by drinking the magic waters regularly, found relief for their stomach ailments and various other maladies.

As the river narrowed, it grew more shallow. If the Swans could withstand the job of pushing through all the damage upriver, they might reach their goal. They could travel even into the bright of evening hours. They made camp on flood-cluttered gravel bars and caught grayling from the river to conserve their supplies. Nestled in the comfort of their canvas tent before sleeping, Thomas faithfully recorded the events of each long day in his diary.

Days passed with no sign of a hot springs. The struggle with the ancient river continued. Where the river was shallow the brothers waded, pulling, guiding the boat safely over rocks and debris. At times, the men carried the boat. They were exhausted. July came and went. The second week of August they reached the North Fork of the Chena River and for some unknown reason, turned up it, even though it flowed with less water than the main river. By now Robert's right arm was almost useless. He could barely stand the pain. Should they give up the search? Somewhere ahead they should see steam rising from the mysterious pools where Robert could soak his pain away. No, they would search until they found the Hot Springs, even if it took all summer.

At the mouth of Monument Creek they found even less water and their struggle grew dire. The entrance to the valley was only about a quarter of a mile wide. The creek banks drew inward, as if pointing a way for the brothers. The secluded valley ahead appeared to have been spared the cruelties of nature and humans. Graceful birch and tall spruce trees stood guard along the creek banks. Now and then, the brothers spotted a delicate tamarack (eastern larch) tree. Robert and Thomas continued poling, as cool air descended with the setting sun. All they heard was an occasional ripple of water against the mossy banks or the slap of waves on the prow of their battered boat.

The delta of Spring Creek narrowed again. Waters flowed peacefully until a meadow, protected by the surrounding hills like giant battle shields, came into view. Sunlight cut between wild rose bushes and lush grasses, scattered bluebells, Hudson Bay tea bushes and large ferns. It was paradise. Stacked like firewood on the edge of the bank, freshly cut willow branches and small trees lay in the dark-green moss, limbed, ready to be dragged or floated to wherever the beavers wanted them. Other willows, not limbed, lay as they had fallen, work abandoned, the chewing apparently interrupted mid-bite. They could not see the beavers' lodge from the boat but a stick and mud dam backed up the creek, channeling waters into a stand of nearby trees. This side-pool probably provided a moat of protection for dens camouflaged by trees. The underbrush rustled with wild creatures scurrying through their summer rituals, sensing the approach of their fall deadline.

The Swans grounded their boat on the bank and continued on foot up Spring Creek. Suddenly from the trees and the hillsides, a choir of calls sounded. Were the brothers being welcomed, or were the denizens of the trees warning their friends of their approach? The birds weren't in flight. As suddenly as the calls began, they stopped. The brothers heard a haunting call above the valley as a loon dove toward earth. When the Swans looked upward, they saw what they had only imagined for weeks. Steam—and fog!

The mist rose above the tops of the trees in thick, white clouds, drifting into the dark blue evening sky as the two brothers scampered through the trees, energy renewed by the thought of a hot bath just ahead. As the Swans neared their journey's end, the loon yodeled a shrill warning, but the men found their treasure.

On August 5, 1905, Thomas and Robert Swan emerged from the dense forest and walked onto a meadow on the upper Big Chena watershed, 125 river miles northeast of Fairbanks, in the Alaska Territory. There, nestled near the cool running waters of Spring Creek, pools of hot miracle waters bubbled with promise.

CHAPTER 2

Expectations

Spring, 1954

The old airfield across the street from Denali Elementary School was the site of a housing development. Weeks Field once buzzed with airplanes between Fairbanks and the outlying villages. But now the old field was dotted with young birch trees bearing new leaves of spring, now slated to become a city park. Had it been a clear day, I would have been able to see a faint outline of Mt. McKinley peeking over the southern horizon, but the sun shown through a haze. The mountain hid behind the mist.

I wasn't very far from the other side of the field when I accidentally stomped into a puddle, suddenly splashing cold water onto my face. The icy smack brought me to a standstill in the middle of a large pond of melted snow. The spattering of black water soaked the front of my white sailor's blouse. My long curls, now damp, clung to my face while Mom's stern words to me when I left for school that morning bumped the walls inside my head. "Your father's coming home for supper. Stay out of the mud, Gwennie. Keep your clothes nice."

Any other spring day I would have lingered on my way home from school to search for signs of life in the dirty run-off. Today, however, my twelfth birthday had finally arrived. As soon as school let out, I ran for home, along the muddy path across the old field to the shortcut through the woods, still trying to think of the place our family might be going. My brothers and I had been given no hints about our destination. All my father Carl would tell us was that our family would leave when school was out for summer. He said we had to guess where we were going. He wouldn't tell us the big surprise until dinnertime on my actual birthday. It had to be a very special place since Carl had been acting so secretive about it.

I grabbed the hem of my navy blue skirt, wiped off my mud-streaked glasses, shoved the thick lenses back onto my nose and slowly stepped through the mud to the other side of the field. Cold water flooded my red rubber boots and trickled down to my toes. Knots from my stomach crawled up my throat and stayed there. Now I was in big trouble!

I proceeded along the cement walkway, past the pastel-colored apartment buildings to the Denali store. The air held a chill. The sun could not see the banks of snow still hiding between the old frame apartments, but I could tell the berms had shrunk from how they looked that morning. They were still peppered with black soot that had fallen from the chimneys all winter, but like magic, the snow banks had receded already. This silent but obvious change reminded me of what Carl always said about the coming of spring break-up in Alaska: it calms the mind, takes away winter's harshness, and prom-ises sunlit nights, warm weather, camping trips, fishing and picnics.

I thought it was possible the trip had something to do with my birthday, but I still wondered where we were going. For weeks I tried to think of a place, ignoring the warnings from Mrs. Parent for me to pay attention in class. I loved to daydream about all the places we had been, and places we had never been, but mostly I thought of locations we probably would never go. School did not seem nearly as important as my birthday.

As I walked, the water squished in my boots, reminding me of the spring when the Chena River flooded the backyards across the street from our house. Those yards disappeared under the water for several days. Mom told us not to play there until the dirty water was gone. Mom was always telling us not to play in dirty water. She said we'd get sick. I was without a doubt in very big trouble. I jumped the muddy stream at the bottom of the hill across from the Denali store and headed into the patch of woods.

In the small area of willows we called the wood, Joanne Bachner and I picked bluebells, wild roses, violets, yellow buttercups and cotton grass. Big, fuzzy buds of pussy willows were the first to bloom in spring, thick along the narrow path through the thicket. I climbed the brushy bank to the one lane dirt road, leaping over puddles and ruts full of slush. At the bend in the road at Ninth Avenue I wished for brand new shoes because I hated the ugly brown oxfords I always had to wear just because the doctor said so.

At the vine-tangled gate that Carl built between our yard and Joanne's, I shook my skirt. I decided the trip must have something to do with my birthday. Rocky and Terry wouldn't care where we went. All they wanted to know was if they could take their new twenty-twos. I had no doubts about whether my turning twelve was worthy of such secrecy. After all, a girl's twelfth birthday sets in motion the celebrated journey of becoming a young lady. I imagined I would see some miraculous transformation before the day's end, like when a caterpillar grows beautiful wings and soars gracefully into the sky.

Here I was soaking wet, in muddy clothes, not feeling much like a butterfly. As I walked around the corner of the garage, my stomach started squirming like the fat worms I found under the flower garden rocks I overturned every summer when we lived in the house on the corner of Eighth and Kellum. So far my twelfth birthday was not at all like the unfolding of a magnificent new creature.

Mom unlocked the back door and smiled. "Happy Birthday, Gwennie. Did you have a good day at school?" Her blue eyes were brighter than usual and her reddish-brown hair shinier. Today, a blush of pink colored her cheeks, ears and lips.

My younger brothers, Rocky and Terry, stood at attention by the water jug near the entrance to the kitchen and gawked at me. The dog poked his head around Rocky's leg and wagged his long, shaggy orange and black tail.

"Yeah," I said to Mom, hoping the scoldings from Mrs. Parent had not reached her ears. I forced a smile and kissed her cheek, then dropped my schoolbooks on the floor under the coat hooks. I plopped onto the hall rug and fumbled with my boots, waiting for whatever was supposed to happen next.

Belle and Carl Wilson in Fairbanks shortly after making the decision to buy into and become operators of the abandoned Chena Hot Springs.

Mom's dress smelled faintly of bath powder and perfume. It was the dress with all the cheerful colors— the one she only wore for special occasions. Not as special as the coat-dress she wore to my piano recitals but she still looked beautiful. If Mom had noticed my muddy clothes she sure didn't show it.

I knew I was in trouble for ruining my blouse and skirt, but if I had been allowed to wear long pants to school it wouldn't have mattered if my clothes got muddy. It was Carl who didn't like pants. He didn't even like them on Mom; she only wore them when we went hunting, or on picnics.

"There's cake and ice cream!" Terry screeched, his face turning red. Rocky poked him in the shoulder with his elbow. Terry's blond hair always looked whiter when his face got red. I could tell they knew where my present was. My brothers looked like they were going to explode, with their puffed-up cheeks and muffled snickering.

The boys always looked alike, in matching plaid shirts and rolled-up blue jeans, and always home from school before me because I was the oldest and had more responsibilities. Rocky was two years younger than I, but a year older than Terry.

I couldn't ask about the trip again. It wouldn't be polite. I set my boots side by side on the newspaper against the wall so as not to slop up the floor. Still, no one said a word about my present. Totem stared at me with saggy brown eyes, slithered to the rug and pushed his cold black nose onto my face. I wiped my cheek with the back of my hand and patted his head. Even when Totem was in trouble, he wagged his tail.

After a long silence, to the very last second when I didn't think I could remain polite any longer and would have to ask about the surprise, Mom chirped: "Your present is in the basement, Gwennie." *Why did I have to go in the basement for my present?* I wondered. Rocky and Terry snickered, their mouths twisted into weird grins.

"Your father will be here soon and then we'll have supper." Mom paused and spaced out the next words very slowly, looking at me with one eyebrow cocked. "You'd better take a bath and change your clothes before he gets home."

Before drawing a bath, I forced myself to walk to the basement door and opened it one inch. What could possibly be down there that was connected to the trip and my birthday present? I could feel my arms and legs stiffen as I thought of the creepy darkness from my least favorite place in the whole world. My stomach curled into a knot. The furnace was silent. My brothers watched from the open doorway. Totem peeked from under Mom's skirt as she flipped on the light. Rocky and Terry leered at me like I was headed straight into a trap they'd had a hand in setting. I stepped down the steep, narrow stairway into the dimly lit dungeon for Slubbertails—waiting for one of those imaginary creatures of the deep to grab me.

Underneath the stairs, behind thick, stringy cobwebs and fuzzy black stuff was where They waited. Only the canned beets and watermelon pickles were stored there. It would have been a perfect place to play, but from the time we moved into the house I'd heard noises and knew we would never be able to play there safely. The boys had no idea what I knew.

On cold winter mornings in the kitchen, my brothers and I would lie on the heat register under the mangle to keep warm. (Every Saturday morning, Mom would press clean tablecloths between the mangle's heavy metal rollers.) I could hear the Slubbertails, monsters of the dark, dragging themselves through the metal passages beneath the floor. As noisy as it was, the heat register was never as frightening as the basement. Luckily, the square holes in the floor vents were too small for wild creatures to snag my foot and drag me down.

My present must have something to do with the furnace, I thought. Just before the heat came on, I could hear moaning and rumblings and sighing and clicking from inside the dirty, big green box on the other side of the stairs, as the Slubbertails raced inside before the big puff from the fiery box burped out its heat. When the furnace was cool, I could hear the creatures come out to play. I had never actually seen them for myself. I was never sure when the furnace was going to ignite, but I knew if I were ever down in the basement near the stairs when that happened, the Slubbertails would certainly clutch my legs so I couldn't escape.

I was cold. My legs shook with every step downward. Bracing myself on the walls of the narrow stairway, I descended nearer the floor. *Any minute*, I thought, *They will grab me and I'll be done for, on my birthday, of all days.* On the last step, I groped for the cement floor with my foot and then tiptoed into the dimness, my curiosity battling an ugly terror. I tried my best to ignore the shadows, focusing on feeling around for a big box tied with a bow.

A flash of yellow glittered. Double thumps beat inside my chest. On the other side of the basement, coal-black fur sparkled in the shadows against the gray wall. Two eyes blinked.

I wanted to run.

Four eyes blinked. Could I make it to the stairs before the furnace came on?

Dusty rays of daylight squeezed through a hazy window. Further down, in the rumpled blankets on the old bed Carl had shoved against the cement wall, I saw two tiny kittens.

I raced to the edge of the bed and picked one up, holding it close to my face, stroking his soft, black, velvet-like coat. They looked alike except the bigger kitten had white hairs under its chin. They were so small and cute, looking up at me with shiny, big, yellow eyes.

"You're not a Slubbertail," I said, listening to its buzzing purrs.

Halfway up the basement stairs with both kittens cradled in my arms, I remembered the dirty green box. I scurried up the rest of the way and slammed the door shut with my foot before They could get me or the kitties.

∽

All through dinner, Carl grinned like he did whenever he had a secret.

"We're going hunting," Rocky said.

Carl shook his head.

"Fishing?" Terry asked.

"Nope. Not even close."

Carl laughed and a playful expression drew his eyes to slits. "I'll tell you when we have cake. Since it's your birthday, Gwennie, you and the boys can stay up late."

Since I had already had a bath, after supper I put my pajamas on without being told and sat next to Carl at the kitchen table. The boys were taking their bath now. I still couldn't figure out how the kittens had anything to do with a trip, or my almost-teenager birthday.

There'd been trips before, lots of them. One time we went to Steele Creek in the Forty Mile to visit Uncle Woody and Aunt Ruth and their beautiful golden-haired cat, Pandora. The cat perched on the counter near the metal cage of the old post office, like it was guarding the mail. On another trip, we took a ferry ride across the Yukon River to the old town of Dawson when Grandma and Grandpa Wilson came for a visit. We always looked forward to driving to Palmer, Alaska (where my brothers and I were born) to see Nan and Bill, because we got to stay overnight in an old log roadhouse, and I felt like a settler. We always took hunting trips in the fall. Our longest trip was the journey "outside" to the Lower 48, to see Grandma and Grandpa Heller in Seattle then Grandpa Wilson on his ranch in Wyoming.

I re-counted the candles on the cake in the middle of the table. There were twelve pink candles all right, each one poked into a white glob of frosting. My mind kept trying on new ideas. I knew the kittens couldn't ride with us to Seattle, and it wasn't hunting season. I was never allowed to miss my piano lessons except for hunting trips or the time we went to Seattle. So where could we go where the kittens could go and what could be so important enough for me to miss piano?

I sat there in my clean, dry pajamas, staring at the flickering candles and let out a sigh. Twelve was not feeling so magical. My special day had turned into an ordinary day, but the mystery trip made up for my disappointment. Mom stacked the dirty dinner plates and wiped off the table.

Carl shuffled through a pile of papers clipped together. We never called him Daddy. Mom said when I was learning to talk I managed the word "Carl" and he thought it was cute. From then on, my brothers and I called him Carl. I feared that before the evening ended there would be a little "talking to" in store for me about getting my clothes dirty that afternoon, but he hadn't mentioned mud all evening. I dreaded his lectures.

Water splashed in the bathroom and I heard the boys giggle. The back doorbell rang, and Carl got up to check.

"Come on in," Carl called to his good friend.

Chuck Gray was loaded down with books and papers. He looked through dark framed glasses at the kitchen table as he leaned against the kitchen doorway. His light brown hair was never messy, not like Carl's.

"We're about to have some birthday cake," Carl announced, sliding the cake from the center of the table until it was directly in front of me. He gave me a wink.

"Heard anything yet about a break-up, Chuck?" Mom asked.

"No, nothing yet." Chuck sat down on the bench across the table from me. He rummaged through the books, set a brown paper bag to the side and flipped through the clipped-together papers Carl had given him. "I brought everything I could find, I...."

Carl raised a finger to his lips. "Later," he whispered, sitting down on the bench next to Chuck. "The boys are still in the bathtub."

Chuck nodded his head like he understood. "Happy Birthday, Gwennie." He set his books on the edge of the table.

Charles Gray was handsome, several years younger than Carl, but still almost thirty, officially old. He worked at the local newspaper, the *Fairbanks Daily News-Miner*. Chuck had been a bush pilot for six years. He and Carl often went hunting together. Three years earlier, at age 23, Chuck was the youngest person ever licensed as a hunting guide in the Territory of Alaska.

I eyed the books. They were black and looked important. There was also a stack of maps, which puzzled me. My birthday party was supposed to be just our family; no one mentioned Chuck was coming, even if he was a close friend of the family. Now I really wanted to know what was in the paper bag.

Chuck smiled. "The ice could break tonight. Wouldn't that be a big surprise?"

I nodded.

I liked to drive along the Chena River and stare at the tripod that local contest officials set on the ice below the Cushman Street Bridge. I wished as hard as I could the ice would bust apart and topple the tripod right then while I was watching. When the tripod tipped, a slack line to a clock drew taut and stopped the clock, marking another spring break-up for Interior Alaska. But choosing the exact hour to the nearest minute the clock stopped was tricky, and everybody watched the weather like hawks before placing their bets. Carl always chose the day of my birthday but in the eight years we had lived in Fairbanks he had never won. The Tanana River Ice Classic at Nenana, established in 1917, was even bigger. A few years after World War II ended, the jackpot for Nenana's contest was more than $100,000. Break-up was a big deal because it meant the arrival of spring, when riverboat travel and tourism of the Last Frontier could resume for the year.

The boys scurried from their bedroom in their matching ski pajamas and climbed up to the table, smelling like soap.

"Figured out the surprise?" Carl asked them. Rocky and Terry shook their heads and poked each other in the ribs. Boys.

Chuck handed me the brown paper bag. His pale blue eyes twinkled when something inside jingled. I unfolded the bag and pulled out two small leather collars. Each one had a tiny silver bell. "For my kittens?" I asked.

Mom lit the birthday candles and Carl danced a two-step to the entrance of the kitchen to flip off the lights. The red light glowed on the coffee pot as it perked away on the kitchen counter, but everything else was dark, enough for candles, anyway. I squeezed my eyes shut to make a wish, then glanced at Chuck. *He must know where we are going*, I thought. *How else could he have known about the kittens?* I blew hard at the dozen candles and wished for new shoes.

"So, where are we going?" Terry asked, shoving a hunk of cake into his mouth.

"It's sort of a camping trip," Carl said. "Don't talk with your mouth full."

"Can we take the twenty-twos we got for Christmas?" Rocky asked.

"We'll see," answered Carl. "Remember when your mother and I flew up to dynamite the ice floe in March, how the big snowstorm stranded us for a few days at the old mountain resort?"

I'd seen the pictures Carl had taken. Even if I hadn't, he told the story so many times I could imagine it. Monument Creek had overflowed its banks and was inching its way across the snow-covered dirt airstrip, freezing layer upon layer, nearing the back door of the old lodge. If Carl hadn't blasted the ice jam apart, the ice would have damaged the building. What most intrigued me were the old things Mom found: dishes, sheets, pillows, towels, blankets, furniture—even some food, but it was all old. Things were left behind as if someone had walked out one day and never come back. While waiting three days for the plane to come, Carl and Mom ate the canned soup and pasta he found in the cellar under the lodge. What an adventure! I wanted to see it for myself.

Carl and Belle Wilson standing in front of the airplane that flew them to Chena Hot Springs in March 1954 to inspect the property as a possible investment.

Carl said, "That's where we're going, the old Chena Hot Springs resort! We're going to clean it up and get it ready to open for business by the Fourth of July. We're staying all summer." With eyebrows high in delight, he looked at each of our faces for a reaction.

"All summer?" I couldn't believe it.

"What's a hot springs?" Terry asked, face smeared with frosting. Chuck was grinning, glancing at Mom. Rocky sat motionless, staring at Carl, his mouth hanging open.

"Better close that mouth, Rocky. Might catch some flies," Chuck teased.

Gradually everybody started moving again. Mom passed the napkins and served the coffee. We kids got mugs of hot chocolate with mini marshmallows.

"Long ago," Carl began, "prospectors, miners, and residents of Fairbanks used to travel with horses and sleds over the old winter trail. Some used dog teams to get to Chena Hot Springs, but at first they used the river. A few walked. After a time, some roadhouses were built so travelers could stay over and continue the journey the next day. They soaked their bodies aching from rheumatism in the hot mineral water that bubbled up from deep in the ground. In those days, crossing the frozen rivers on a winter trail was easier than it would be today. These days, the only way to get there is by airplane."

"Is that how we're going?" Rocky asked.

"No, we're taking the swamp buggy and the D4 Caterpillar. We'll need the equipment to get the resort running, and we'll need the jeep and trailer to haul gear. You kids'll want to finish your classes strong but there's a lot you can do to help us get ready in the next few weeks before we leave." He paused, looked at me and grinned. "We're going to have to make a special box for those new kittens to ride in, Gwennie." I clapped my hands in excitement.

"What about Totem?" Rocky asked.

"The dog can go, too," Carl said. Rocky cheered. Terry blew steam off his hot chocolate, his mouth still outlined in frosting the color of his hair.

Without a word, I left the table and went to my bedroom. I never dreamed I would get to go to an old resort, let alone help run one. It wasn't even one of my guesses. I would never have gotten the kittens if we weren't bound for the hot springs; Mom would never have allowed it. I wondered what we were going to do with Tweety-Bird.

I grabbed my comb and brush and the little box of bobby pins from my dresser and glanced in the mirror. I looked exactly the same as I had looked that morning except for my droopy long finger-curls. My special day had not transformed me, but now I had other things to think about.

I scurried back to the kitchen where Carl and Chuck were unfolding the maps and surveying the trails. The more they talked, the more excited I became.

"It'll be tough for the D4 this time of year," Carl said. "That old stage trail winds up the Chena River Valley for over sixty miles." He said the trail was nothing

The Wilson kids pose at their home at Eighth and Kellum Streets shortly before they left for a new life at Chena Hot Springs in May 1954.

but swampland at the lower end and had too many river crossings. Traveling would be easier if he took the equipment in from the Steese Highway over land rather than following the winter trail they said George Wilson used in his later years, before World War I. Carl studied the map.

I leaned over the table for a closer look at the map. "Who's George Wilson?" I asked.

"Sit up straight and stop fidgeting," Mom said as she secured a pin curl tightly to my head. Rocky and Terry giggled. *They're too young to understand what Carl's talking about. They're just glad they get to stay up past their bedtime.*

Mom wrapped another section of hair around two fingers and pinned a fat curl to my head with three black bobby pins. Every morning she combed the pin curls into picture-perfect, long ringlets that spiraled down past my waist. I wanted a ponytail like some of the other girls at school, or short hair without any curls, but Carl didn't like ponytails so every night Mom rolled and pinned my hair for school.

"I want to haul the D4 to the campsite the week before we leave town," Carl said. "Don't think the wagon trail is the best way to go."

Chuck nodded. "Looks like leaving from Faith Creek would be an easier route." He unfolded another map. "It's higher country, fewer crossings. You could start down nearer the mouth of Faith Creek on the Steese. We could fly over the country and check out the hills before you make the drive."

Carl liked that idea. Chuck knew a lot about everything. He hunted many parts of Alaska, so he knew about sheep, moose and caribou, and the terrain they roamed. His knowledge surpassed many of the best outdoorsmen in the Territory.

Chuck drew a line on the map with a pencil and marked "Xs" along the line as he spoke. "Mt. Ryan, Frozenfoot Creek, West Fork, North Fork, junction of Monument Creek. It'll take you a week if you follow the ridges. It's only twenty miles from Faith Creek to the big hill near the Hot Springs."

Mom pinned up the last curl and I scooted next to Carl on the other side of the table. "Who's George Wilson?" I asked again.

"He homesteaded Chena Hot Springs," Carl said.

"Is he related to us?"

"No," Carl laughed, "just had the same last name. George was from Canada. Built most of the old cabins up there for the first people to stay in."

"Are there any horses up there?" asked Rocky.

"Not now, but the old stable is still there." Carl grew quiet, gazing out the window. "It's been almost fifty years since the Springs were discovered."

"What else is up there?" Terry asked.

"There's a big dining room and a swimming pool. We'll live in the old lodge."

Rocky nudged Terry with an elbow. "A swimming pool!"

Terry's eyes grew wide as bowls. "We'll get to go swimming?"

"A story, please tell us a story," I said.

"Yeah, more about Chena Hot Springs," Terry said.

"I bet they had guns back then," chirped Rocky.

"One story, then bedtime," said Carl, setting his coffee mug on the table and drawing a deep breath.

33

CHAPTER 3

The First Bathhouse

"I was almost dead. I had rheumatism all through me. My right arm was
so bad I could hardly move it. I had been doctoring here...taken all kinds
of medicine, and it done me no good."
– Robert M. Swan

A bright warm morning followed the Swan brothers' discovery. They
had located three hot springs on the left bank of Spring Creek. They
also found a fourth spring, much larger than the others, on the right
bank. Robert and Thomas awoke early to scout for logs in a nearby
stand of spruce trees. Swallows flew everywhere; green and blue, their
wings fanned the wind as they circled, investigating the new human
activities. Robert's rheumatism had worsened on the trip upriver so
Thomas did most of the labor.

The air reeked of sulphur. Thomas chopped, limbed, and dragged
many logs to a spot near their tent on the left bank of Spring Creek.
After several days of toil they had enough logs to build a crude
bathhouse over one of the hot pools.

Bubbling to the surface of the land from below the black earth,
the hot mineral water had formed large pools and carved numerous
cooler run-off streams that ran into Spring Creek. Robert and
Thomas dammed off one part of the creek to run into a pool where
the cold creek water could temper the hot mineral water for a

comfortable bath. They lined the pool with stones. To protect the pool from weather and animals, they built a shed over it. On August 15th, Robert took his first bath.

The bathhouse was small, just big enough for the pool and a ledge for dressing. The stones were almost too hot for bare feet. With every passing day Robert grew stronger, taking two, sometimes three baths a day. While he soaked he listened to the echoes of Monument Creek rushing on the far side of the valley, to Spring Creek rippling nearby, and to the chortles of a loon's mating calls. After fifteen days of relaxing in the medicinal springs, Robert combed his hair with his right hand, a bit of grooming he had not been able to do for months. He and Thomas breathed a sigh of relief seeing this silent miracle.

The brothers knew they had to return to town. September was just around the corner and the rivers would soon freeze. But as the leaves changed color and fluttered to the ground, the men continued to soak in the dug-out tub under the log bathhouse, delaying the trip as long as possible. They drank water from the hot springs every day and took long, quiet walks. They found game trails. Chunks of charred wood in an old campfire pit were the only sign that another human walked the valley.

One night while the Swans slept, someone slipped into their camp and stole their food. The next morning as they packed up to leave, four Italian prospectors approached their camp. While working four miles upstream, they had been robbed, too. Since the discovery of gold, crime had become more commonplace in the Interior, but this particular day of theft was likely the work of Charles Hendrickson, the notorious thief in a blue parka.

Earlier that summer, a rash of looting and hold-ups in Fairbanks and nearby mining communities put the town in a panic. Mr. Hendrickson became somewhat of a legend. Bundled in a blue parka, he managed to elude the Fairbanks authorities time and time again. It wasn't until the latter part of June that he was caught, but then used an iron hoop saw to cut the jail bars. "The Blue Parka Bandit" soon returned to his thievery.

The jails couldn't hold Hendrickson. Manhunts couldn't find him and the frequency of highway robberies had Fairbanks citizens ready to take matters into their own hands. When the story leaked to the papers "Outside" Alaska, as to the way law and order was not being kept in Fairbanks, the matter embarrassed the townspeople.

The Swan brothers prepared for the trip back downriver to Fairbanks. On a scrap of wood Thomas carved their names, along with the date they arrived, and nailed it to the bathhouse door.

The next spring, Aaron Van Curler, a local miner and prospector, learned about the Swans' discovery. He told the brothers he wanted to join their return trip to the hot springs, because his wife suffered from rheumatism and stomach trouble. Robert, also, longed to go back to the hot springs. His arm was not entirely healed.

Weather was hot and dry, hotter than any spring since the building of the town. The settlers had persevered through extreme hardships, facing a gauntlet of elements they would just as soon forget—floods, extreme cold, and food shortage.

Now came the fire. Near the end of May, a blaze broke out in the center of downtown Fairbanks. The fire started in a dentist's office when a gust of wind lifted a window curtain onto a kerosene lantern. In a mere forty minutes the fire consumed the dry, wooden buildings between First and Third Avenues, from Cushman to Lacey. The only building left standing in the business sector was the Northern Commercial Company warehouse, which held nearly all the town's food supply. The last of the flood damage from the year before had only recently been repaired.

The Swans, Van Curlers and the rest of the townspeople faced a heap of smoldering ashes where there once stood a vibrant downtown. Rebuilding began even before the black, sooty mess could cool. Every hand was needed.

Not until July 28, 1906, again by poling boat, were the Swan brothers free to return to the hot springs—this time, with Mr. and Mrs. Van Curler and their friend, Mrs. Moody. This trip was much easier because the swift river flow had cleared last year's flood debris, and because the Swans were now familiar with the course of the winding river. They reached the valley of the springs the second week of August.

Van Curler was amazed to see the bubbling pools and lone wood structure Thomas had built. The crude bathhouse was badly weathered, but intact, with his wooden sign still nailed to the door. Apparently no one had been there since they left. This year, however, their company included another man and two women, so the bathhouse was too small. The men fashioned a lean-to and dug out a larger bath, so all could enjoy the water every day. Every night, while a candle dripped, Thomas faithfully noted the day's activities in his diary as was his custom.

In September, the party poled back down the river to Fairbanks, Robert and the two women almost completely cured. The Swan brothers never went back to the hot springs again.

CHAPTER 4

Departure

———

May, 1954

Three days after my birthday, at 6:00 P.M., the ice went out in the Tanana River at Nenana. Carl missed winning both ice break-up jackpots yet again but he didn't seem to care. His enthusiasm was intense, as if we were leaving the very next day and everything had to be done by morning. School would be out in less than two weeks, but the day of departure felt a long way away.

Carl was home a lot and all he talked about was the trip to the Hot Springs. Early Saturday morning, he and Chuck flew over the routes they discussed at the family party. That evening over supper Carl told the family we would leave from Faith Creek on the Steese Highway and approach the resort beyond the mountain ridges, above timberline.

"I figure we'll need two weeks of groceries," he said, "one week of food for the trip in and food for another week when we get there. Chuck said he would fly more in when we get there."

"So how will Chuck know when we get there?" Rocky asked.

"He'll check on us every so many days with his plane. Belle, did you know Cap Lathrop wanted to buy the old resort at one time?" Mom shook her head no.

"Can the kittens come upstairs later?" I asked.

"Not tonight, Gwennie," Mom said, "and dishes before you go downstairs."

Terry chimed in. "Me, too. I want to see the kitties, too."

Carl went on. "Cap told me he even had a plan to build a road from Fairbanks into the Hot Springs by following the old winter trail. Guess when Cap changed his mind about the purchase of the Springs, he dropped the idea of a road."

Cap owned the theaters and a lot of other things in Alaska. I was four years old when I first met Captain Lathrop. He was tall, with thick, white hair that tumbled down his forehead like a snow berm. When he said hello, his eyes danced like he had a surprise. Later, when I was older and visited Carl at work, I saw Cap bring famous people into the theaters he owned. He always took them up to the projection booth to meet Carl and carry on adult conversations that I listened in on.

Carl was head projectionist at the Lacey Street and Empress theaters and usually ate supper at work, so the boys and I took turns delivering it. Mom carefully arranged covered dishes of hot food and goodies wrapped in wax paper, all in a dark red bag with big handles she made on her sewing machine. During the week Carl ran the afternoon matinees and late shows. On Saturday nights after the shows, my brothers and I ran up and down the empty rows of seats collecting lost belongings, dropped coins, empty popcorn bags and torn candy wrappers.

Sometimes I got permission to stay at work with Carl. He showed me how to splice the ends of film together. I watched carefully, so when the light in the corner of the movie screen flashed I pushed the button on the control panel. If the next reel of film streaked onto the wide screen without missing a frame, I got a silent nod and a big smile from Carl.

Back at home, I stacked the clean dishes from the dishwasher on the counter because I wasn't tall enough to reach the cupboards. I listened to Carl tell the boys about all the river crossings up the old trail. He said that the number of river crossings made traveling almost impossible during the summer months. We could use the trail during the winter, but only after the rivers froze solid and only if the trail were plowed of snow. I helped Mom clear the table.

Mom stopped in thought, leaning up against the counter. "Y'know, five weeks isn't very long to do all the work there is to do before the Fourth. It will take at least a week just to scour out that filthy old kitchen."

"How come?" Rocky asked.

"People fly in, stay overnight, and don't clean up. The lodge looked like somebody had one big party before your Dad and I got there in March," Mom sighed.

"It wasn't *that* messy," Carl said. "You have to remember the years that place stood vacant without anyone at all living there."

"It's not right they come and go with no one minding the place, Carl. People should have more respect for things that don't belong to them."

"Most people do have respect, Belle. There just wasn't anyone up there to remind them to watch their manners. It won't take long to clean it up. We'll all pitch in," he reassured her.

"Probably in worse condition now," Mom muttered, more to herself than to anyone else. She carried the plates and silverware to the sink.

"What's a 'verse addition'?" asked Terry.

"Worse condition. Pay attention. Stuff all over the place." Carl shook his head.

Mom faced the sink, her back to the table, as she rinsed a plate off from supper. She smiled, handing it to me to stack on the counter.

"What stuff?" I asked Mom. She knew I was listening to every word, even while we took care of the dishes.

"Garbage, junk, old things—empty bottles, dirty pots and pans. You and I will have fun looking through all the old things."

I let my mind wander on all the treasures we might find in the rustic lodge. When the dishes were done I led the way down the narrow stairway into the basement. Terry carried the bowl of leftovers. The kittens were waiting for us, hunched together on the bottom step. The new collars fit perfectly: the brown one for Topsey, the black one for Holly. Their whiskers and tails were strewn with cobwebs, a sure sign they had been tracking Slubbertails under the bed, around the furnace, in corners, and probably into the hole in the wall. I had no doubt the boys' commotion kept the Slubbertails out of sight. Topsey would outgrow Holly someday soon, with that monstrous appetite of hers.

In the weeks that followed, Carl and Mom assigned projects for all of us. I tackled my chores after school with an eagerness I didn't know I was capable of. I emptied the dryer, folded clothes, ironed hankies and dishtowels on the mangle. Mom even let me iron the boys' shirts.

A week before we were to leave town Mom lined up her lists on the kitchen counter in neat rows like salmon on the drying rack: pack clean clothes, buy groceries, pack food. She checked and rechecked those lists daily, drawing a straight line through each task she completed, adding details and projects she forgot to put down the first time. When her notes filled up one list, she pulled out another memo pad and started a new one.

"You boys sweep out the garage while I'm gone," Carl told Rocky and Terry the morning he hauled the D4 Caterpillar to Faith Creek.

The boys stood elbow to elbow, nodding their heads slowly. They were almost the same size because they were only fourteen months apart. Strangers thought they were twins because Mom dressed them alike. After Carl left, Mom had to tell them three times to straighten up their room, they were so antsy to get going. Instead of doing their room chore, they carried camping gear from the basement to the garage. While they readied the supplies, Mom and I drove to the Northern Commercial Company to buy groceries. When we got back with the groceries, Carl was already back, sitting on a chair, watching Rocky and Terry sweep out the garage. He was still tired from the trip with the Cat.

Mom and I had strolled slowly up and down the aisles of the Northern Commercial Company. Mom stacked the cart neatly with towers of canned meat, soup, fruit, vegetables, milk, and butter. "Nothing must be forgotten," Mom said, checking off items from three of her lists. By the time we got to the last aisle the cart was piled above the edge with provisions for the big trip. Most items needed only water to prepare: pancake mix, plain flour, instant coffee, orange juice, cocoa mix, Kool-Aid, powdered milk, powdered eggs, and dried potatoes. Then there was the fun stuff: sugar, bread, graham crackers, marshmallows, soda crackers, Corn Flakes, Rice Krispies and oatmeal, plus Crisco, Kleenex, dog food, soap, cat food, toothpaste, and toilet paper.

All three of the Wilson kids were born in Palmer, Alaska and moved to Fairbanks in 1946. Gwen went to school at Denali Elementary through the sixth grade. Shown here is Rocky, center, and Terry before the two of them started school.

Mom arranged to have the groceries delivered to our house, then she surprised me with the purchase of a pair of brand new tennis shoes. She said I couldn't wear them until the day we left for the Hot Springs, but in my room at night when the house was quiet and I was suppose to be in bed, I carefully lifted them out of the cardboard box and slid my feet into them. Perfect! They were bright white, and softer than my ugly, brown oxfords. The heel of the left oxford was built up higher than the right one, to correct the difference in the length of my legs. They made me feel like a freak.

I was positive once we reached the resort I would never have to do exercises again because Dr. Haggland said swimming was the best exercise in the whole world for straightening a spine. Dr. Haggland found the curve in my spine when I was in fourth grade. "Scoliosis," came his verdict, as he handed me a list of exercises to help straighten my back. Every day after school, before I did anything else, I had to do jumping jacks, push-ups, chin-ups, and toe-touches without bending my knees. Mom held my feet down for the sit-ups.

On the last day of school, I rushed across the field for home, report card clenched tightly in one hand. Today the kids at school didn't sing "Skinny Gwennie! Skinny Gwennie!" or point their chubby fingers at me. I felt older than twelve years old, and was sure I looked it.

Down the hill and into the woods I ran, through the secret place where Joanne and I picked wildflowers to tie into pretty bouquets with different colored threads to sell to all the neighbors—ten cents for big bouquets, a nickel for the little ones. That was a lot more fun than selling punch in crumply paper cups for pennies. I felt sad when I realized I wouldn't be picking flowers with Joanne this summer. There wouldn't be anyone to play with but my brothers and I wasn't sure what that would be like. I was going to miss Joanne and our summer adventures.

The driveway was crowded with tools, chains, ropes, shovels, our yellow rain slickers, and Carl's hunting boots. Rocky dropped a sleeping bag on the side of the driveway and moaned. "Carl said we have to go to bed right after supper 'cause we're leaving before the birds wake up."

Carl was sitting in the garage, braiding pieces of twine. Sometimes it was hard to know when Carl was pleased or angry, because when he was silent he could still be upset. Now and again when my friends came to visit, they asked whether he was mad when he was quiet. I couldn't say, since I never knew for sure. He might just be thinking about something else. What's more, even when he was upset he still told jokes.

Carl never said a word to me about getting my clothes muddy a few weeks earlier. I'd decided he must be going easy on me because it happened on my birthday. Now I handed him my report card and held my breath, since it wasn't my birthday. He tied a knot at one end of the braid and attached the cord to the top of the kittens' box to hold down the screened top. He took ahold of the report card and his eyes roved back and forth, across the yellow page. He didn't speak.

Carl handed the report card back to me. "Next time, how about an 'A' or two?" He didn't smile.

I nodded and stood waiting, then realized that was the end of the discussion. I walked back into the house and changed my clothes. That wasn't so hard. Maybe the trip was more important than my report card.

I had packed some of my things weeks earlier: Nancy Drew books, my Girl Scout Handbook, my diary, the Bingo game, clothes, and the little cedar box I kept stationery in, so I could write to Grandma Heller and Joanne. Uncle Lyle and Aunt Pat were coming by later to pick up Tweety Bird. They were going to watch the house while we were gone. I wondered how big my new bedroom was and what it would be like living so far away from town, without electricity, roads or shops. Since Carl had told us about George Wilson and the old trail to the Hot Springs, I found myself wondering what living at the Springs must have been like so long ago, and whether it would be different now.

I pictured myself in a horse-drawn double-ender sled all dressed up in a long fur-trimmed coat with a matching hat, huddled under layers of blankets, as the horses pulled the sled through deep snowdrifts, up the wind-blown trail to the grand Lodge. The roadhouses along the way would smell of wood smoke. The low, yellow flame in the old-fashioned oil lamp would give my room a warm glow, while an oversized water pitcher and hand-painted washbowl sat always ready on a wooden stand. After washing my hands and face, I would join the other travelers near the crackling wood stove at the entrance of the roadhouse. In my mind, we gathered around a long, rough-hewn table for a supper of steaming peas, corn and green beans with bits of bacon, mashed potatoes and gravy. There would be oval platters loaded with fried chicken and thick, juicy moose steaks, grilled and served by the kitchen help. Outside, safe and warm for the night, husky teams would sleep burrowed in snow banks, or curled up inside tiny doghouses of logs built by the roadhouse owners. With tummies full, humans and huskies alike would sleep soundly.

When I had changed my clothes I shook off the fantasy and headed down to the kitchen to help Mom roll up two dozen eggs in newspaper and return the eggs to their paper cartons. Mom tucked the cartons under a stack of dishtowels in one of the metal food boxes.

"Those eggs better not break before I crack them," she said with a wink, as she closed the lid.

The next morning a cloudless sky displayed a wide-awake sun. The army jeep and swamp buggy pulled out of our driveway at 5:00 A.M. and quietly rolled down Eighth Avenue to Cowles Street. Carl and the boys led with the buggy, its open bed loaded with barrels of diesel, gas, tools, and camping gear. Before we got past downtown, Totem panted like he was already tired. He stretched his neck over the back of the swamp buggy, sniffed the wind several times, turned a couple of circles, then snuggled into a tiny space near the rear of the buggy. Mom and I followed in the jeep, pulling the over-packed, two-wheel trailer covered with a canvas tarp that Carl had wired tightly in six places. Cuddled together on the back seat, slept Holly and Topsey, in the special box Carl had made.

Our steel caravan maneuvered through the streets of the sleeping town, turned left at Cowles Street and headed for the Chena River.

At First Avenue we turned right and followed the riverfront to the Cushman Street Bridge. We crossed the bridge over the Chena River, and I thought, *there's where the Swans started poling up the river 50 years ago.* Murky gray water slid underneath the bridge, like it always did when it wasn't frozen. The airplane tires on the army-green buggy rolled onto the narrow, gravel road that led out of town.

I could see Fairbanks from the rear window of the jeep as we angled around Birch Hill. The sleeping town hugged both sides of the Chena River, sprawling along the banks like two open fans. The morning sun struck the river water, bounced off in silver streaks and lit up the steel bridge between Cushman Street and Slaterville, where Chuck Gray lived. First Avenue wound along the river. The shiny tin siding on the Northern Commercial Company, once Captain Barnette's old trading post, looked like glass in the morning light. I saw the stately Masonic Lodge, our favorite ice cream shop, the studio where Mrs. Popovich held dance lessons, and the old log library on the corner of Cowles and First. All these familiar places waited, so quiet in the morning light, while we trundled on past.

The stores and hotels had faced the river that way for fifty years but the days of filling gold pokes with rich yellow metal from the ground were about gone. Carl said Fairbanks was now the take-off and supply point for the Arctic, whether civilians who hunted, trapped or fished, or military personnel stationed at the nearby bases. "People who live here are still tough; they have to be. Alaska is a tough place to live and those who aren't tough leave."

I leaned my head against the window as our vehicles jogged up the Steese toward the campsite and the waiting D4 Caterpillar. Faith Creek was a long way away, but I didn't care. We were on our way to Chena Hot Springs. I had new shoes and for the first time in forever Mom and I were both wearing jeans.

CHAPTER 5

Faith Creek

We followed the gravel of Steese Highway for hours, 81 miles to be exact, farther and farther from town, with its friends, bicycles, and weekly piano lessons. Away from stores, electricity, hot and cold running water, heat registers, Slubbertails, washing machines, dryers, and dishwashers. No more delivered water jugs or milk bottles, mail or groceries. No telephones, neighborhood squabbles, or evening drives through the streets of town after taking Carl his supper. We were going to Chena Hot Springs, and I couldn't believe it.

A near midnight sun hung in the distance when we pulled to a stop on the edge of Faith Creek country. The setting sun draped the wide valley with spellbinding radiance, like glowing orange paint. Carl stared at the valley for a long time without saying a word, then pointed to the ridges in the distance. "That's where we're headed. Tomorrow we build a trail so we can drive the jeep and swamp buggy to the base of those mountains." What he called mountains were mere bumps, much smaller than I had imagined. But it was high country above timberline.

Carl dragged the heavy canvas tent from the back of the swamp buggy to the bank of the noisy creek. Rocky and Terry grabbed sleeping bags and water buckets. Carl unfolded the tent.

I couldn't take my eyes off the mountains. The sea of noiseless spruce trees was turning black before my eyes in the late hour, as shadows filled the space between our camp and those mountains.

Spooky. Except for the birds and animals that were probably sleeping, we were alone. The air smelled like Christmas trees, a happy and familiar scent, but I wanted to see the creatures that must be hiding in those deep woods.

Mom rummaged in the food boxes and I handed Carl the tent stakes. He pounded the last stake into the rocky ground and crawled through the doorway that was hidden in the folds of green canvas, dragging tent poles behind him. The tent swelled up like a huge frog.

For the next two days the D4 Caterpillar penetrated the Faith Creek wilderness. When he wasn't working the bulldozer, Carl gave the boys and me a lesson on how leaves, water, and peat-like matter had built up for years to make the compact clumps hidden in the hollows of the land surface. The incline and the bogs required long hours of work to clear. As the yellow D4 battled the bushy tussocks, I imagined the clumps as heads of jungle warriors hiding in the shin-deep carpet Carl called sphagnum moss.

Mom usually stayed near the tent. At first Rocky and Terry rode the tractor with Carl, but on the morning of the second day camping, Terry woke up complaining of a sore throat, so Carl told him he had to recuperate in the tent. Terry started bellyaching and hurled himself onto his sleeping bag, with added drama, for effect.

"Muskeg," Carl said during lunch, "is taking longer than I expected. Got to get the Cat through that stuff first. When we get to the mountains, it'll get easier."

I believed him. We all did. By late evening the trail was still not complete. Mom told me to go tell Carl that supper was ready.

The spruce trees grew densely packed. Even in the bright of day, within the limbs of spruce it was as dark as late evening. I hadn't roamed far from the trail Cal was building, and already I squinted into the darkness, fearing what might be lurking among the dark, droopy branches. I could tell Mom was annoyed by another late night of keeping supper warm.

I ran across the upturned ground to where Carl and Rocky had worked most of the day and told them it was time to eat. Carl said he would be along shortly, so I sat on a moss tussock to wait for him and watch the sun resting on the rim of the world. I waited for more than an hour, thinking Carl would shut the Cat off at any minute. When he didn't, I concluded he must be working late so we could leave for the mountains in the morning. The hopeful thought kept me cheerful when it would have been easy to give in to the frustration.

I listened to the groans of the yellow bulldozer hidden within the spruce trees and tried hard not to get irritated. The night sun from an orange-blue sky turned the spruce trees blacker, and the heat of the day sank into the moss beneath me. Soon the sun would climb the northern sky and start a new day.

Not once in the past two days had Carl gotten cross with us. The black soil and wet moss halted the D4's progress many times, yet Carl seemed to turn the problem into a game. He always told me you must never quit. There's always a way. It's like a race with yourself.

The enormous sprockets on the D4 held the wide steel tracks in place. Carl tried to keep the tracks cleaned out so the debris wouldn't build up and dislodge a track. He'd climb down from the driver's seat, clean out the muck, pull out any spruce limbs jammed in the tracks, pop the tracks back into place with a crowbar, and climb back up into the saddle. It seemed like an endless battle.

When the grunting of the D4 tapered to a purr, I played the echo game I'd made up the day before to see if I could guess when Carl was going to shut off the tractor. The D4 grew louder. He had opened the throttle wider, till the valley throbbed and the pounding changed to banging and the mountains echoed back wildly. He changed gears, and the drone of the earthmover swelled like a lion's roar as it cut through more unturned tundra.

The black boughs of the spruce trees surrounding me looked like a long, wide canvas, etched and feathered with dark, green paint by a famous artist. Millions of spruce boughs, pierced by sun-rays of oranges, yellows and blues, encircled the bog, while the distant mountains seemed proud to stand alone. I snuggled deeper into the moss and thought of swimming and fishing and hiking once we reached the Hot Springs. I could write letters by the light of lanterns, or by the glow of candles like the trappers and miners of "yesteryear," as the adults would say. I was sure it would be more fun than riding bikes and picking flowers.

The kittens! I hadn't checked on them in a long time. *Carl will eat supper when he decides to,* I decided to believe. I retreated to the tent.

My never-again-so-white canvas shoes skimmed the tops of dirt clogs, while up top, my long pigtails, ends secured with rubber bands, flopped across my back. I hated pigtails. They were ugly. I looked back at the wall of spruce for a glimpse of the D4, but saw no sign of it. The scent of spruce needles, curly moss and moist earth from the melting of the top layer of ice in the tundra smelled fresh and full of promise.

How could a valley like Faith Creek be so pretty and ugly at the same time? *This valley has its own rules*, I thought. *It even fooled Carl.* I reached the creek and began following the gravel bar back to camp when the wails from Topsey and Holly pierced the night air. There was no sign of Mom or Terry.

"Mom, I'm back!" I yelled, running on toward the jeep. My chest heaved in and out for air as I fumbled for the string and the bent nail on the top of the kittens' travel box. "You haven't been out of here the whole time, poor things!" I raised the screen.

The kittens peered up at me from a soft bundle of coziness, where they napped on each other. Gladly, the cats had not messed in their box. "It's okay," I said in my best baby-voice. The kittens scampered from the box to the front seat of the jeep, and down to the rocky ground, pretend-attacking each other as if they were big jungle cats. I sat on the rocks near the tent and watched them run circles around camp—free, full of cooped-up energy, backs arched, black tails slicing the air while the yellow D4 behind the stand of spruce trees bellowed and cut away more of nature's wooded hideaway. The quiet tones of Mom's voice came from inside the tent and I guessed Terry was worse.

Puffy, pink clouds streaked a near midnight sunset. I thought of sticky cotton candy at the Tanana Valley Fair when leaves drop and the sun disappears for almost the whole day and I whispered to myself *he's probably almost done now*. A firm roar from the D4 rolled across the valley and faded beyond the mountains. Holly darted between the airplane tires of the buggy that looked like a fat pickup. The Cat fell silent.

From inside the tent I heard a puff from the Coleman stove as Mom reheated dinner. I gathered up the kittens and put them in their box. *Tomorrow*, I thought. *We're leaving tomorrow. I hope. I hope. I hope.*

Over supper, Carl discussed going back to town. Later as I tried to go to sleep, uncertainties about leaving for the mountains in the morning whirled in my head. The longer I pestered myself about it, the more worried I became. My brothers were already asleep. Mom was finishing up the dishes from supper and Carl seemed deep in thought, resting on one elbow on the floor of the tent with a cup of coffee and looking sad.

Carl was 21 years old when he left Wyoming for Alaska. He said his thirst for adventure was inherited, in his blood. He loved to tell the story about the Wilsons immigrating from England over 200 years ago, with James Oglethorpe who founded the Georgia colony, to "mend the wounds of indebtedness in the motherland." Oglethorpe was a famous British social reformer who wanted to give poor people who would go to debtors prison a fresh start overseas, where they could work on family farms to support the new colony, giving back to society instead of turning to crime, a big problem in London at that time. None of Carl's family knew for sure if the story of traveling to the New World in the 1730s with Oglethorpe was true. They joked about it. His grandfather told stories of the family in bits and pieces to Carl as a youngster in Oklahoma, relaying family history through stories that had always been passed on.

Before the American Civil War broke out, the Wilson family migrated from Virginia to Kentucky and on to the White River in Missouri. There, land was plentiful and life prosperous. However, when the Civil War started, Carl's great-grandfather enlisted in the

Confederate Army and left with General Price. Later, with permission to return to the White River to move his family out of danger, a gang of ruthless men claimed by neither army nor civilians murdered Great-Grandfather Wilson while the family watched. Later Carl's grandfather moved his wife and children into Indian Territory, called Oklahoma. When he grew up, Carl's father moved his family to Wyoming and built a homestead house of logs. The struggles with the land and hardships of the 1930s Great Depression were severe but as Carl grew up, his father repeated the same stories of Wilson family history whenever they gathered around the fireplace in their house of logs.

"I'm going to need more diesel for the Cat," I heard Carl say.

The lid of a metal food box slammed. I peeked through slits to see Mom leave the tent with the pan of dirty dishwater. I shut my eyes and crossed my fingers extra hard and wished for the high ridges in the morning.

"Belle...." Carl said when she returned.

I peeked again. By the light of the gas lantern, Carl's white tee-shirt glowed, almost hypnotic. He had grayed early in life. Under a bright sun his hair was the color of salt and pepper. Tonight, it sparkled in the light like tinsel draped on a Christmas tree. Mom sat down beside him, rubbed lotion into the back of her hands. Carl put his arm around her and drew her close.

"Belle, in the morning, you and Gwen better take the jeep and drive back into town with Terry."

Terry was half hidden in one corner of the tent, curled up under folds of the feather-filled, zippered sleeping bag. I closed my eyes and tried to figure out how long it would take to get to town and back.

"We'll be here awhile longer before I have a trail we can drive on," Carl said.

I knew it. The spruce trees and moss are getting worse. Our small D4 is not quite up to the job.

"See if the doctor will look at him," Carl said, "and have Ken send more diesel up. With more fuel and what we have left, we should be okay. We'll make better time once we get to high country."

"I dread a trip back to town," Mom said, "but if we don't, and Terry gets worse after we leave the highway, we will wish we had. His throat looks better, but he feels warmer."

Carl talked on about living at the Hot Springs and how he had always tried to improve his station in life and wanted something better for the family and for him. He turned off the Coleman lantern. In the light of pre-dawn, Faith Creek rippled on its well-worn course to a much larger body of water.

"Big Chena Hot Springs," Carl said, quietly. "The gold played out, the horse and buggy disappeared, the old trail grew to weeds, but that hot water keeps right on bubbling."

In the diffuse light of early morning, the once grand meeting place of another era seemed like a place unlike anything I had ever known, yet a place we would call home this summer. Even though Carl was worried about the time lost with the trail battle at Faith Creek he was excited about the trip across land and getting the resort open by the Fourth of July. Maybe we could make up the lost time even if we weren't going to arrive in the time he planned.

"It must be the greatest feeling in the world to be able to discover such a place and develop it, watch it grow," Carl said. "The resort hasn't seen the hustle-bustle of activity since the early days, and no one else made a go of the Hot Springs the way George Wilson did." Carl said he would have liked George Wilson.

I decided the drive back to town would take a whole day. We'd probably have to stay the night at our house and stay another day so Terry could see the doctor and another day to drive back to camp. I didn't want to go back to town. In the morning I would ask if I could stay at camp with Carl.

Faith Creek gurgled on, and we slept.

CHAPTER 6

Road of Trials

———

Carl was singing when I woke up. The likeness of a cross bounced along the floor of the tent.

"Where's Mom?" I asked him, rubbing sleep from my eyes.

"Mom's at the creek. Hey, Rocky! Terry! Come on. Everybody get up. Time to get dressed. Breakfast's almost ready."

I had never seen Carl act so comical, let alone cook breakfast. The cross shadow, cast by the intense morning sunshine streaking through a design on the mosquito screen draping the doorway, danced, as Carl, armed with a pancake spatula, swished his fanny from side to side and sang his favorite song, "I'm Headin' for the Last Round-Up."

I was wide awake now and suddenly remembered the conversations from the night before, about having to go back to town. I sat straight up in my sleeping bag and looked at the boys. Rocky's dark, curly hair was all I could see of him, curled up in his sleeping bag. Nearby, Terry was lying flat on his back, halfway in his sleeping bag. His eyes were closed. His blond hair shimmered in a sunbeam. He didn't look very sick to me.

Carl lifted bacon from a small frying pan with a fork and spooned four circles of pancake batter into another pan. He looked back over his shoulder to see if we were doing as he had asked.

"Time to rise and shine," Carl said. His tone of voice meant right now, then he went back to singing.

"Don't look! Don't look!" yelled Rocky, then Terry. I said I wouldn't and covered my eyes with my hands. The boys reached for their blue jeans. Beyond the tent the forest swelled in the harmony of birds performing their ancient morning routines.

The boys pulled on their jeans, stuffed their shirttails into their pants, and left for the privacy of the trees with toothpaste and toothbrushes. Terry was big for his age. In the winter the boys wore plaid flannel shirts and matching flannel-lined jeans. In the summer they wore cotton shirts and unlined jeans. Mom stitched an "X" in black thread onto all of Rocky's clothing so she could sort the laundry more easily.

Soon Terry wanted a special "X," so she sewed double "Xs" in all his things. Everything had one or two Xs: she marked two cowboy hats, two cowboy guns, two toy tractors, two toy cars. This past Christmas it was two twenty-twos under the tree, each with one boy's name printed on the gun butt in bright, red nail polish.

It was fun to watch Terry's face turn beet red when he got mad. He would puff and stew and holler at Rocky and me about all kinds of things, but his complaining was only important to him. Eventually Rocky found that if he remained quiet long enough while Terry yelled, he could seize the right moment to tease him with obnoxious rhymes.

"Gwendolyn!?" Mom called, walking into the tent. "Get dressed." She gave me one of her "I mean business" looks and put her toothbrush and toothpaste in the tray of her train case. It was always "Gwendolyn" when she was firm with me. I shoved my jeans into the sleeping bag. With one good yank I had them on in no time.

"I'm dressed," I announced, crawling out and posing like a model, one hand behind my head, the other on one hip. "Can I stay here with Carl, and not go to town? Please, Mom. Please?"

Mom methodically spread her washcloth over the top of the stove lid to air dry and smoothed out the wrinkles with her fingertips. Even out here in the wilderness she kept things neat. She turned and stood next to Carl, watching him flip pancakes in midair. I quickly rolled up my sleeping bag into a sloppy ball, drew up the cotton cords to secure the bag and tied a poor excuse for a bow. I left the tent mumbling through toothpaste foam, "I don't want to go back to town."

Alert spiders skimmed the ripples in the creek and scooted under the grassy bank to get away from the birds' clicking beaks. I watched the birds criss-cross back and forth between the creek banks and into the treetops carrying pieces of twigs and grass in their beaks. Near the riverbank, colonies of tiny white flies moved together in a miniature tornado above the gravel bar. A multitude of century-old rituals had been triggered that morning and the sun climbed a path toward heaven to watch.

From the banks of Faith Creek and into the woods, as far away as the mountains on the horizon, the tiny brown and gray sparrows that had followed us from Faith Creek hunted for weed seeds. Chickadees fluttered near the wooded areas around camp, their black-capped heads still covered for a winter storm.

I brushed my teeth as three camp robbers—Canada Jays and magpies—dove close to the tent watching for scraps of food, then screeching and bickering among themselves. Why did Terry have to go and get sick? Going back to town was not to my liking.

We left for Fairbanks directly after breakfast, with Terry sprawled over the back seat of jeep, Mom and I in the front. Carl said he would have a trail to the new campsite completed by the time we got back. Gladly, the return trip to our house in town seemed shorter.

Early the next morning Mom called and ordered more diesel and set an appointment for Terry with Dr. Haggland later that afternoon. We returned to Faith Creek the following evening as Carl and Rocky arrived back at camp on foot.

"We left the D4 at the new camp, three miles out," Carl said. "How's Terry?"

"As long as he takes this medicine, Dr. Haggland didn't see any reason for us not to continue on. He said we are undertaking an 'unbelievable trip.'"

"And the diesel?" asked Carl.

"It should be here tonight."

Morning would bring the start across the valley with the jeep and buggy, so falling asleep was tough for me. Once we left the Steese Highway, we would be alone. Thinking of it was eerie. Old George Wilson building a cabin in the middle of nowhere, with no one to talk to, must have taken a lot of nerve. Even the Swan brothers, when they finally arrived at the hot springs, probably thought that all their hard work polling up the river was worth the trouble and could talk to each other about it. I couldn't wait for Carl's next story.

I awoke early in the morning and rolled up my sleeping bag, this time making sure I rolled it into a neat bundle. I helped Carl cook breakfast, then followed him around camp doing whatever I could think of so we could leave sooner. Everyone pitched in to gather, pack, carry, and load supplies from the tent into the trailer and the swamp buggy. With extra fuel delivered the night before, additional space was hard to find in the buggy bed, but somehow, we made room for everything. Totem panted from underneath the swamp buggy and watched for a signal from Carl to move. I secured Topsey and Holly in their box.

All morning our caravan pushed through uprooted growth toward the distant mountains. I checked Topsey and Holly often to make sure they were all right but they were always cuddled up together and the jerky ride didn't seem to bother them. Carl and the boys led with the buggy. Mom and I followed with the jeep and trailer, and as we crawled forward, I watched the mountains up ahead grow bigger and bigger.

We spooked two moose from the underbrush just before lunch. The moose didn't seem to know what was happening. We were nearly on top of them before they trotted off, crashing and banging through the bushes, ears flat against their heads, eyes buggy, with the longest legs I had ever seen prancing over swamp bogs and scraggy spruce. They never looked back.

> Visit June 15 1967 — Thurs.
> at home, unpacked, etc. Terry
> HOME from Brooks. DR SAID to Soakin'
> SpRiNgs wateR. Best medicine !..
> Terry walked from end of Road !
> July 2 1967 Sun. Horse Packers Left 3pm
> FoR FAR MouNTAiN
>
> July 2 Mom + I to town for Freight
> Tommy RobeRTs walked up. He + Terry
> Went fishing — !!
> July 4 People, People, People

Gwen not only kept a diary, but also wrote stories about daily events. Shown here is a page from her diary in 1967 after returning from an Oklahoma college to work at the springs during the summer. She chose this page in honor of her brother, Terry, who had just spent three years in Army hospitals recovering from wounds received in Vietnam.

Twice we stopped for snacks and drinks, and took trips "for privacy" into the woods as needed. Totem maintained a steady pace alongside the jeep. His tongue flopped out the side of his drooling mouth and from time to time he trotted to the other side of the trail to drink water from the ditches. Seldom did he break his pace or wander far. What a good dog.

Mom winced with pain when the steering wheel whipped to the left and to the right from dirt clogs hooked on a tire. Soon she used a looser grip, letting the steering wheel slide through the curvature of her fingers. Before long she was steering around the dirt clogs, guiding the creeping jeep forward along the uneven ruts made by the

D4. It seemed an endless, winding course. It was late in the evening before we reached the new campsite.

The relay system repeated the next day. First, Carl cleared a trail with the yellow bulldozer. It was a struggle to level the black earth and Carl stopped often to fix slipped tracks. When the crude trail was completed, he walked back to the waiting jeep and swamp buggy, then he and Mom advanced the vehicles further into rougher country. The boys and I carried rocks out of the path of the wheels, throwing them to the side of the trail. Creeping, bumping and jerking, we made our way north. The route grew more difficult as we reached higher country.

The D4 now had to tow the swamp buggy and jeep up the steep inclines, so steep I feared the vehicle would flip over backwards. I knew Carl wouldn't give up. No matter how long it took, or how difficult the route became, we would never turn back.

On the afternoon of the third day out from Faith Creek, the beautiful dense woods and thick green moss lay behind and below us. Carl halted the caravan at the edge of the treeline on Mt. Ryan. There was nothing ahead but bare slopes stretching into the sky like ghost roads.

I scrambled out of the jeep and stood beside the vehicles. The ridge where I stood joined a higher ridge further up the mountain. Mt. Ryan was the biggest mountain I had ever seen, like a gigantic wall without a door, reminding us that regardless of our family's plans, the forces of nature had the final word. I was surprised when Carl said we had only come six miles.

"It's hot for May," he said.

I let the kittens out of their box to run in the fresh mountain air, free of dirt and grime the giant tires of the buggy had been kicking up ever since we left Faith Creek. Mt. Ryan was really big. I tried to figure out how we were going to get over the top of it. It was a dismal thought.

"I hope these clear skies continue. May is not a month for heavy rains, but we're overdue for some," Carl said. He wiped his brow with the back of his hand. "We've got enough to deal with without having to battle spring rains on these slippery side-hills. We've been lucky so far."

Terry whined. "Are we going to eat now? I'm hungry."

"Maybe this would be a good time to shoot the twenty-twos," Rocky said.

"Gwennie, get me the map off the Cat," Carl yelled from the jeep. The boys wandered off. When I returned, Carl was sitting with Mom on the hood of the jeep, chewing on a little twig. I handed him the map. He pushed his hair, damp with sweat, back from his forehead. Deep, dirty lines extended across his brow. He frowned at the ridge above us and told Mom he would walk back.

When the boys returned he motioned for them to follow him. The three of them took off on foot up the steep ridge of Mt. Ryan. Totem followed wagging his tail between his hind legs. What Carl had said about walking back confused me. I watched the three of them climb the side of the mountain until they were the size of pencil dots. I hopped up beside Mom on the front end of the jeep knowing that having to wait through another delay would be frustrating.

"What did he mean about walking back?" I asked.

I didn't expect an answer to my question. Decision-making conversations between her and Carl were never repeated to me or the boys, and when Mom and Carl did make a plan Mom only explained briefly, saying things like she didn't know for sure, or your father isn't sure. She usually omitted the stuff I really wanted to know.

Carl and the boys looked like ants crawling on an anthill, black specks moving slowly up the mountain.

"Your dad thinks this ridge is too steep for the swamp buggy and jeep to make it on their own power. He wants to leave the swamp buggy behind."

Carl always said if a plan doesn't work out the first time, you choose another plan to reach your goal. Were we *quitting*? Wilsons don't quit. We're tough.

"Gwennie, get your brush. I'll fix your hair." Mom tugged through my long tresses, braided two pigtails, and secured each braid with a rubber band. I hated pigtails. Pigtails were for little girls, not 12-year-olds.

Mom was reserved, soft-spoken in the presence of company, and mindful of the manners she had taught me. I hoped when I grew up to be a lady I would be pretty like her.

"If your father has to tow both the swamp buggy and the jeep up these mountains we'll lose more time," she said. "It's taken longer than he wanted just to get this far."

I watched her dab lipstick along her thin lips with the fourth finger of her right hand. She spread the red color evenly, explaining how the long line of independent, brave pioneer women in her family, including herself, had one thing in common––the ability to survive a wilderness yet maintain their femininity.

Mom's great-grandmother crossed into Kansas from Missouri in the 1850s, after she married. Homestead land had opened up to white settlers so she and her husband raised a large family despite the perils of beginning new lives in a new land. Their family survived persistent raids by the indigenous Indians and later, bloody border conflicts during the American Civil War.

In the late 1890s, Mom's grandmother left Kansas with a daughter and three sons, following a cruel marriage and bitter divorce proceedings. They headed for Telluride, Colorado. In the booming but crude mining town where free-spirited miners reigned, her grandmother raised her only daughter alone, cooked at the mines in the summer and operated a boarding house during the winter.

Grandpa and Grandma Heller sailed for Haines, Alaska Territory, in 1914. Gold fever had stricken nearly everyone. Mom, an only child, was born in Haines four years later, then raised in Juneau, among a transient population of fishermen, cannery workers and fortune hunters.

Now my mother faced wilderness survival with her own daughter—me. Like the three women before her, two of whom she had been named for, Mom was teaching me the advantages "ladies" in other places of the world enjoy and how to act like a lady while performing the unladylike duties of wilderness survival.

By the time Carl and the boys hiked off the mountain, Mom had given me a complete lesson in lipstick application, sitting there on the hood of the jeep. Rocky and Terry reached the jeep pointing fingers and calling me names, till I said I needed to wash my face. I was crushed. I didn't have permission to wear lipstick and the tiny mirror in the powder compact must have failed to reveal just how funny I looked. Even worse, Carl didn't notice my giant but quiet step toward womanhood. *Never mind all that*, I thought.

We unloaded the swamp buggy. All the while Carl and Mom discussed which provisions we truly needed for the remainder of the trip. We sorted, juggled and separated the supplies before repacking the trailer. We loaded the rest into the bed of the swamp buggy. I helped rope and wire the gray canvas tarp over the back of the swamp buggy while Mom talked about hungry bears, the hams, and the only slab of bacon.

"It won't be long now, will it, before we're there, I mean?" I asked Carl.

"Let's get going," he said. "Want to get more ground covered before we camp."

"Those beautiful smoked hams," Mom sighed. "I hate to leave them behind."

"There's no other choice," Carl said with a wink. "Won't be long now," he said to me.

Carl connected a heavy chain from the rear of the D4 to the front bumper of the jeep. Rocky and Terry rounded up Totem. The kittens whined and wiggled to get loose when I lifted them into their box.

The D4 inched up the steep slope toward the bald dome of Mt. Ryan. The powerful bulldozer coughed and sputtered as it jerked the jeep and trailer forward up the winding route Carl and the boys had scouted earlier. I looked back at the swamp buggy, barely visible in the scraggy mountain brush near the bottom of the slope. The buggy looked lonely, forgotten. The scene brought to mind a movie I had seen of a pioneer mother in a covered wagon looking back at her trunk she had to abandon alongside the trail. They could only bring the essentials.

This is a new plan, I thought. Even so, I couldn't take my eyes off the swamp buggy as it shrank behind us, less and less significant. Finally it disappeared altogether.

That evening, high above the timberline on a slope of Mt. Ryan, the wind slapped the sides of the green canvas tent in and out. The day had exhausted everyone. We ate a quick supper of creamed tuna and peas, then cleaned up the dishes. The boys wriggled into their sleeping bags. Mom and I took a "girls only" walk. When Carl returned from his stroll, he tied the tent flap securely over the door.

"How did George Wilson find Chena Hot Springs?" I asked, slipping into my sleeping bag.

"George had heard of a hot springs up the Chena, while he was still in the Yukon," Carl said, unlacing his boots.

"What was George like?" I asked.

Mom unrolled her sleeping bag and scooted inside.

"A smart man," Carl said, as he took his boots off and set them on the floor near the end of his sleeping bag. "George was prospecting for gold on the Middle Fork of the Chena River. The hot springs were northwest of the mining camp. George figured walking a straight line to the hot springs from DeMars Creek would be shorter than following the river." Carl crawled into his sleeping bag.

"Is that when he homesteaded the Hot Springs?"

Carl said no and fell asleep. No matter. I wasn't far behind.

CHAPTER 7

George W. Wilson

*"The whole north hill is mostly covered with long grass, native grass.
I found no frost, only a little on the surface. It was all thawed ground."*
– George W. Wilson

George William Wilson was born March 14, 1870, in Port Sarnia, Ontario, in the Dominion of Canada, about a one-and-a-half miles north of Michigan.

Sarnia faced the city of Port Huron, Michigan. The two cities were separated by the St. Clair River, which flowed into Lake St. Clair and on into Lake Erie. East of Sarnia, the town of Petrolia became the hub of an intercontinental refining empire. Five miles south of Petrolia, at Oil Springs, were North America's first commercial oil wells.

George's father was Irish, and his mother, Canadian. George grew up and attended school in Ontario. Known as "Soo," Sault Sainte Marie was George's last place of residence in Canada. On June 15, 1889, at the age of nineteen, George left Canada for the United States.

George took the Canadian Pacific Railway to the port of Sault Sainte Marie, Michigan, U.S.A., its Canadian twin town. He lived and worked in the United States for the next several years, seldom visiting his homeland. According to his Declaration of Intention (July 26, 1909) George was restless with life in Michigan, so he left for the gold fields, hoping to make his fortune in the Yukon or Alaska Territory.

While prospecting in the Yukon, George learned of the hot springs on the Upper Chena River. "Old Man Murphy told me about them when I was in the Yukon. He claimed to have been there in '98, I believe."

By 1899, George had found his way to Alaska (Statement of George Wilson, Feb. 27, 1912). The following summer, on July 5, 1900, he sailed into Homer, on the Cook Inlet.

∽

The summer of 1907 found George on the Middle Fork of the Chena River northeast of Fairbanks in the company of other hopeful prospectors. Fairbanks was booming. The Fourth of July celebrations were going to be the biggest ever, since scores of men in the mining camps were availing themselves of the new 45-mile narrow-gauge train and the special holiday rate for the trip to town.

A telegraph line had brought Fairbanks and the outside world closer together. Stage service between Valdez and Fairbanks hauled passengers and supplies, and the city council had big plans for a new school. There was a bookstore, several hardware and cigar stores, jewelry stores and hotels. The Sunday band concerts featured nearly every state in the Union as well as several other nations.

The miners and prospectors arrived at the depot on Garden Island across the river from town and headed for the grandstand between Cushman Street and the Fairview Hotel. There was plenty of food, games, a parade and fireworks. Speeches reminded everyone of the founding of the country and the wars fought to protect it. All gave thanks for their part of the world—and for the gold.

Judge Wickersham had successfully established a court system in Alaska. However, the arduous travel and battles with dishonest scallions netted him new enemies and made his work more difficult. President Teddy Roosevelt had kept Wickersham in office with recess appointments, but a new man would be in the White House soon. His supporters doubted whether Wickersham would have the same kind of support he had grown accustomed to. Wickersham considered running for Territorial Congressional Delegate.

Meanwhile, E. T. Barnette was popping his vest buttons over the growth of his trading post. Backed by Seattle money, Barnette founded the Washington-Alaska Bank and was its president. His bank was thriving, but Barnette was repeatedly written up in the newspapers for shifty dealings. Trouble was also brewing in the miners' meetings and there was talk of striking.

❧

That Fourth of July in Fairbanks, the townspeople gossiped about the Swan brothers and their discovery on the Upper Chena River; everyone was curious. A hot springs near Fairbanks would be closer than Manley Hot Springs down the Tanana River. Manley's springs were homesteaded about the time the U.S. Army Signal Corps set up a telegraph station in Fairbanks, so the public was now fully aware of its existence.

Fairbanks experienced two major fires in the early days, but was quickly rebuilt after this fire in 1906. Scene is looking upriver past three docked riverboats. *(Courtesy Albert Johnson Photograph collection, Alaska and Polar Regions Collections, Rasmusen Library, UAF.)*

Other than Manley, the only other hot springs lay over the mountains from Fairbanks near Circle City in the Yukon River drainage. That area was homesteaded the year before, but was a long trip by river or by pioneer trails across the Tanana hills. Both popular hot springs were far away.

Earlier that summer, George Wilson, Aaron Van Curler and a dozen other men with high hopes prospected for gold on the Middle Fork of the Chena River. Large operators had been successful around Fairbanks. Gold production the year before hit over $9 million.

Out of curiosity, George and Charlie Mack, another prospector, left the Middle Fork and took off on foot across country to explore, their intrigue aroused by rumors of a hot springs on the North Fork. With well-stocked backpacks, the two men blazed a trail from DeMars Creek through the wilderness, found a low pass over the hills separating the two forks of the river and located Chena Hot Springs.

The small bathhouse built by the Swans was still there. In the mineral-rich soil around the pools, salt-hardy redtop grass grew thick, as high as their hips. George and Charlie inspected the weathered log bathhouse. The extreme moisture and heat trapped inside had begun to rot the logs. And the smell! The musty deterioration and stench of sulphur sent George and Charlie back out into fresh air in short order.

The secluded valley and wooded hills of birch and spruce trees was astir as the two men set up their camp along Spring Creek, upwind of the stink. A flock of noisy swallows inhabited the meadow. When the two men settled down for the night by a small campfire, the swallows fell silent, roosting in the nearby birch trees and on the bathhouse, guarding their territory.

In the days that followed, George walked the land. About 800 feet from the hot springs, he knelt down and dug several inches into the dirt, in thawed ground! Surprised by what he found, George began digging other holes. In Fairbanks and the surrounding area, he knew seasonal thawing would not go very deep. The permafrost common to interior Alaska was often 100 feet thick, but here near the hot springs, there was no permafrost.

The interior of Alaska enjoys a short and sweet growing season. To grow crops successfully in such an extreme climate, early farmers had to remove the top layers of moss and insulation, then thaw and till the soil before planting. By 1903, the Tanana Valley successfully supported abundant crops of cabbage, lettuce, potatoes and other root vegetables. Many Fairbanksans also had private hothouses for raising more delicate produce like tomatoes. Despite the short 90-day growing season, the prolonged hours of sunlight spurred the growth of extraordinarily huge vegetables, and still does to this day.

George Wilson had never considered settling permanently in any one place, until now. He would be back.

CHAPTER 8

Mount Ryan

———

May 26, 1954, was a cold Wednesday. Morning rain slapped the roof of the tent. Carl mumbled something about checking the weather. I was eager to leave because by evening we would be close to the resort, so I slipped on a rain slicker and scurried down the slippery slope of Mt. Ryan in pursuit of my father.

On a level, shelf-like grade of land below camp, Carl suddenly turned and faced me. Raindrops ran off the end of his nose. He looked stunned.

"Where did *you* come from?" he yelled through the downpour.

"I don't know," I said.

We stood in the drippy foliage while Carl stared at me in silence, deciding what to do with me.

Where did I come from? What did I do? I thought. *I should have asked if I could go with him.* I looked behind me through the dim morning light. The mighty mound of earth and rock I'd marveled at the day before hid somewhere behind a wall of fog. Yesterday the mountain guarded the wilderness between the Steese Highway and the hot springs. Today not even the sun could see through the white shroud on Mt. Ryan's mighty slopes. The line between sky and earth had vanished.

Carl snapped off a twig from a nearby bush and pulled the leaves off one by one. "I hope we don't have to sit this out," he said. He glared at the mountain and clenched the leafless twig between his teeth.

"Me, too," I said.

The caravan consisted of the D4 Caterpillar, the jeep, trailer and swamp buggy. This was the point at which Carl decided it was necessary to abandon the swamp buggy if they were to make it to the Springs before the Fourth of July. Mt. Ryan is in the background.

Mt. Ryan doesn't like us on his land. He must have asked for the rain. The mountain looked like a fat man sitting cross-legged with a big white hood over his head. *First, Faith Creek, then the swamp buggy... we might be stuck on this mountain for a long, long time.*

"Chances of this clearing today are slim," Carl said, flicking the homemade toothpick from one side of his mouth to the other with his tongue. Rain was an unwelcome factor, maybe halting our progress.

We stood there, getting soaked, while the cold wind blew debris along the drenched surface of the slope, scraping the ground near my soggy sneakers. Some tiny sticks floated down on rivulets between the rocks.

Rain won't stop us, I thought. *Rain can only slow us down. If we weren't at the Hot Springs by the time Carl had planned, Chuck would look for us. Last night Carl said we'd make better time with only the D4 and jeep to manage. He said without the swamp buggy we could make up the time lost. So why is he upset? Why can't we just move on?* My mind went on racing but I kept quiet, because I could see Carl was concentrating.

Wind blew more leaves and trash into the sagging bushes that crouched down against the mountainside. Cold blasts of air shook the tree limbs. Rain beat the hood of my yellow slicker. There were no other sounds—no birds, not even a raven. Nothing.

The rain slid down Carl's troubled face. He stared at the sky, the fog, the clouds and the mountaintop, faintly visible above us.

"So! We're stormed in, huh?" he yelled at the mountain. "Not forever!" He headed back for the tent, up the side of the slope in a brisk stride through the storm soaked, knee-high brush. His arms jerked back and forth as he stomped, and his yellow slicker squeaked.

I knew he had thought of another plan to get us off the mountain before the storm went away. As we walked, Carl said the Fourth of July wouldn't wait for us, whether or not we would like it to. There was too much work to do, to get the old resort open for business— cleaning, ordering food, painting, and repairs. He said we'd have to work hard after we arrived. I quickened my pace to keep up, but Carl's steady stride was too fast. He beat me to the tent.

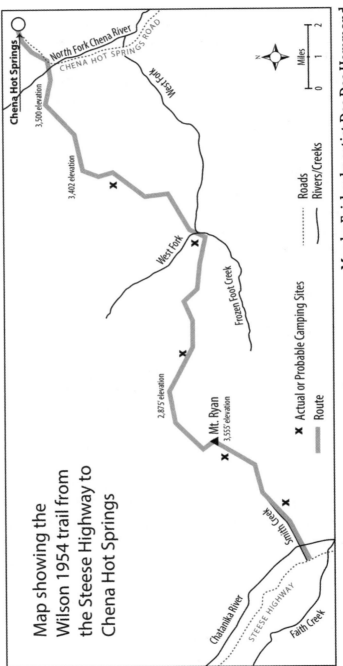

Map showing the Wilson 1954 trail from the Steese Highway to Chena Hot Springs

Map by Fairbanks artist Dee Dee Hammond

When I reached camp, Carl was already checking the trailer to make sure the gear was still dry and the tarp secure. My fingers were stiff from the cold. The look on Carl's face said we weren't going anywhere. I shoved my hands into my pockets and followed him into the tent.

"Wow! It's cold out there," Carl said, pulling the flap of the tent door down behind us. "Any coffee, Belle?" He bit hard on the twig in his mouth, slipped off the wet slicker and put it in front of the door on the floor.

Carl blew into his cupped hands to warm his fingers and sat on the camp stool, flipping the twig from one cheek to the other. "I can't believe we're stuck here. Can't see a thing out there because the fog's so thick," he said as he laughed again. Mom handed him a cup of coffee while I sat down next to him.

Mom lit another burner on the Coleman stove to make oatmeal.

"How long do you think this storm will last?" asked the boys as they rolled up their sleeping bags. Dressed in rain gear and stalling a privacy trip into the wet bushes, they discussed the situation with adult-level seriousness.

"Could last a couple of days from the look of that sky," Carl answered. "Mt. Ryan is not going to make it easy for us." The boys laughed in agreement. They had made it as far as the door flap.

"The side of this mountain's too slippery," Carl said, "too dangerous for the D4. We'll have to wait till it blows over."

The mountain air seemed warmer after breakfast. Finally ready for for the day, Rocky and Terry asked if they could shoot their twenty-twos.

"Not until it stops raining," Carl said. He suggested a game of baseball.

"Gwennie, after the dishes are done, get the water bucket and set it by the tent to catch some rain," Mom said. "Tell the boys we'll have to watch what we use from now on. And tell them no more snacking. That goes for you, too. I'll be along in a few minutes."

Rain rinsed the side of the mountain for the rest of the morning. Not to be kept from enjoying ourselves, we circled the homemade rock bases in our yellow slickers again and again in the wet and cold. When the bases were loaded, the catcher stepped up to bat and made a home run. As time passed, the bucket filled up with rainwater. More rain collected in a camp pan. Mom fixed lunch, then we washed dishes.

∽

May 27, 1954

Thursday afternoon, the rain dwindled to a fine mist by midmorning and the sun tried to come out. Light seeped through two holes in a sky still dark, and deep blue. I could feel the temperature rising. Everyone grew hopeful the storm was showing signs of moving on. Carl gave the boys permission to target practice.

Eagerly, the boys marched side by side along the ridge and away from camp. They cradled the twenty-twos in their arms, gun barrels pointing toward the almost overcast sky, as Carl had taught them. Totem, nose to the ground, trotted near the heels of their black rubber boots.

"We'll leave tomorrow if the weather continues to improve," Carl said, watching Rocky and Terry. "I'm going to walk the side hill and look for a way around to the other side of this mountain."

"Can I go?" I asked.

"Not this time. You stay with your mother."

Mom busied herself with chores after Carl left. I let Topsey and Holly run loose and argued with the bushes why I should be able to go with Carl like the boys when he scouted for routes. I concluded it unfair when girls had to do "girl things." I confided in a big rock that when I grew up I would do all the things I couldn't do now.

After awhile the boys returned and the skies over our camp remained calm until six o'clock, when Mom started supper. The thick canvas sides of the tent began to heave in and out with the gusty winds. I had just enough time to get the cats inside the tent before rain drenched the mountain again.

The rain roared louder than before. Carl did not return.

Totem, Topsey and Holly, content inside where they usually weren't allowed, curled up for the duration. Totem knew he'd better behave himself and stay away from the kittens or he'd be out through the tent flap in no time.

"Where's Carl?" Terry asked. "When's he coming?"

Mom flipped through the pages of a magazine without noticing it was upside down and assured us he should be back soon. She picked up another. The downpour on our skimpy canvas shelter, perched on the side of this big mountain was more proof than I needed that wherever Carl was, he would be better off in here with us than sitting on his heels somewhere out there.

"I hope he comes soon," Rocky said. "I'm hungry! How come he's not back yet?"

"I don't know. He'll be here," Mom said too quickly for me to relax.

The gaslight flickered in a draft. Mom closed up the magazine. I gathered up the cards, put them away and sat close to her, fretting silently that Carl was hurt, had slipped, broken a leg or got lost in the storm. If something did happen I wasn't sure we could carry him back to the tent. I didn't know if we would even be able to find him.

The rain pounded a steady rhythm. The more the wind punched at the tent, the more I was convinced something dreadful had happened to Carl. The boys colored pictures in a *Lone Ranger and Tonto* coloring book. The wind blew harder and Mom told us the storm reminded her of the stormy night she first met Carl in Juneau, Southeast Alaska Territory.

Mom said she liked to watch the ships come and go in Gastineau Channel when she lived in Juneau. The fishing boats left early every morning and returned late in the evening carrying the day's catch. The Navy and Coast Guard frequented the area and passenger boats from Seattle and British Columbia arrived daily. These newcomers to the frontier were bound for adventure, or work, but either way, for a new and tougher way of life. The famous gold rushes at the turn of the century put Alaska on the map, and now, five decades later, people still flocked to Juneau, Anchorage, and inland to Fairbanks.

An unexpected crunch in the rocky ground outside the tent startled all of us. The flap of the tent flew back and Carl stepped inside. "Oh! Thank goodness!" Mom yelped.

Carl's shirt and pants were soaked. He stood there in the doorway grinning, puddles swelling around his boots. The boys started laughing. I'm not sure why, either because they were glad to see him or seeing that his soggy clothes were stuck to his arms and legs and his hair lay flat on his head the same way Totem looked when he swam through the creek the day earlier.

"Where have you been? You had us worried," Mom said.

"I just thought I'd climb to the top of Mt. Ryan. When I reached the top, the fog closed in." He took off his boots. "I couldn't tell which direction was which so I sat down and waited for it to clear up." He tugged off his wet shirt, stepped out of his trousers and stood in the flickering camp light, shivering in his underwear. Mom handed Carl a dry shirt and pants, then dished up supper.

"Found a shovel up on top of the mountain," Carl said, sitting on the campstool near the door of the tent, a plate of food balanced on one knee. "It's still in good condition."

After Mom and I did the dishes we pulled out a deck of playing cards. Carl and the boys made up jokes and everyone seemed more cheery, relieved to have him back in one piece.

"So when did George Wilson go back to the Hot Springs?" I asked, shuffling cards.

"The next summer," Carl said.

"With that guy, Charley?" Rocky wanted to know.

"No, he went alone," Carl said. I saw a smile cross Mom's face, as she proudly laid down three jacks on the sleeping bag in front of her.

Carl went on. "George thought about the rich soil at the hot springs, hoping everyone would find gold on the Middle Fork that summer. If a permanent camp were set up there, the prospecting site would only be a day's walk." Carl put three eights on the table.

"Did they find a lot of gold?" Terry asked, taking a card from the top of the discard pile.

"Probably not as much as they hoped to."

CHAPTER 9

The Homestead

"I located it for a home, to grow vegetables and stuff that
I needed in that country."
– George W. Wilson

May, 1908

As far as George Wilson could tell, no one had been to the Hot Springs since his visit the summer before. The Swans' bathhouse was still standing, undisturbed, though its condition had deteriorated. He stood in the isolated valley, picturing where he would site a cabin and plant a garden. The valley was peaceful, a place George could call his own, rekindling the anticipation he had experienced the year before.

Now almost a year had passed since George had walked into the Hot Springs from the Middle Fork of the Chena River. Everyone's hopes for finding gold on the Middle Fork were stronger this summer. Aaron Van Curler had found prospects on Bedrock Bar, or "Van Curler's Bar," as he called it. As usual, reports exaggerated the richness of the strike, drawing a mild stampede. Every last creek in the vicinity was staked and prospected. Most of the creeks did have gold, but not as plentiful as everyone had hoped. Van Curler diverted the Chena River through an old channel using a large wing dam and shoveled gravel into his sluice box from the bed of the river.

But George was more interested in the richness of the soil on Monument Creek and the Hot Springs. If abundant gold were discovered nearby and a big camp established, it would only be a long day's walk to Chena Hot Springs. He was encouraged to see how close Monument Creek and Spring Creek were to the Middle Fork strikes. Aside from hiking, there was always the Big Chena River, so he could source supplies from Fairbanks by boat. Granted, the trip upriver would be a long one requiring advance planning to make the most of each trip, but it was certainly possible.

According to Wilson's testimony in the 1913 Fairbanks trial, he scouted the area thoroughly for a few years, convinced that homesteading the land on Monument Creek was a grand idea. The warm water heated the earth and he could irrigate in the dry season. There was a freshwater gulch nearby, where the water ran all year 'round, and less frost meant an earlier planting date.

He started by clearing a 50-feet-square area of ground for a turnip patch. Although George was not a citizen of the United States, he interpreted the law to mean that since he had arrived at his adulthood while living in the United States and resided stateside since then, he could be considered the same as a foreigner who had already declared his intention to become a citizen. On May 16, 1908, George posted a location notice for a 160-acre homestead.

At the northeast corner of Spring Creek Valley, George drove his first post into ground. The steel ax-head hit the pole stake, and the knocking echoed through the valley. He continued marking all four corners so the boundary lines could be traced easily, then he headed down to Fairbanks.

Six years had passed since the bright metal of fortunes was found under the frozen moss in some gravel near Fairbanks. The townspeople were still unified; winter activities, holiday festivities and struggles with the elements forged a solid bond between locals. These pioneers who settled the wilderness and happened upon the local treasure were different from this new crop of prospectors who came simply to seek their fortunes. Everyone could feel the growing tension between the two groups. Fairbanks was beginning to lose some of its cohesiveness.

In lockstep with the miners, prospectors and trappers came the lawyers, judges, businessmen and doctors. Scores of ancillary businesses set up offices above the banks, drugstores, and grocery stores. Signs were nailed all over town advertising services and fine merchandise: Northern Commercial Company, Sargent and Pinska Men's Store, and Edgar R. Peoples. A gold strike inevitably meant thriving "pick and shovel" businesses.

Overnight, Fairbanks moved from a humble supply station into a frontier town that lined both sides of the Chena River. The Tanana Valley miners, organized by the Western Federation of Miners, had a rough year with labor demands. Meetings were spied on, Russians were hired to keep ten-hour days going in the mines, and some of the prospectors resorted to violence, with such rich rewards hanging in the balance. Businessmen, not wanting to upset either the operators or their customers, tried to please both. Former Judge Wickersham felt the miners' disputes would impact the upcoming elections. He now practiced law in Fairbanks and was considering running for Alaska's delegate to Congress. E. T. Barnette was still spending a lot of time in court defending his banking practices.

Through the middle of town, a high board fence marked the "Line," a red-light district and a common landmark for locals. Nearby were several dance halls, like The Flora Dora and The Track. On Front Street, where respectable ladies didn't walk and children weren't allowed, many saloons competed with one another. From the diggers' pokes, the ore gradually migrated into businessmen's suit-pockets and their wives' fancy purses. Two-story homes of milled lumber rather than logs were being built with large windows and lovely roof-shaded porches. Flowers bloomed along the walkways.

Unnoticed that summer was the filing of a homestead on the Upper Chena River by a Canadian prospector. George was a big man, nearly six feet tall, and comfortable alone in the woods. He had brown hair, a mole on his right cheek and a dark complexion from long days outdoors, giving him a rugged appearance. A determined individual, George viewed life's opportunities through hazel eyes with cleverness and common sense. Twelve days after leaving the staked-out hot springs, Mr. Wilson strode into the Recorder's Office in Fairbanks to file for a homestead.

Upon being questioned about his United States citizenship, he answered, "I was under the impression that when a boy became of age in the United States that he could get his final papers at any time. That it was the same as a Declaration of Intention" (Wilson Testimony, p. 127).

George's location notice for a 160-acre homestead in Spring Creek Valley, filed at 11:40 A.M. on Thursday, May 28, 1908, stated:

> *"...being declared my intention to become a citizen of the United States of America (sic), I have located one hundred and sixty acres, 160 acres, of unoccupied Government land and hereby claim the same for agricultural purposes and as a homestead, said land being situated in the Fairbanks District, third Division, Territory of Alaska."*

Four months later, George began building his cabin, the first step in seeing his dream of a hot springs resort come true.

CHAPTER 10

Frozenfoot Creek

———

The rain stopped sometime during the night. In the gray morning light, the birds sang their greeting to the new day.

"Want to get going around mid-morning," shouted Carl over his shoulder when he left the tent after breakfast. "Let's give the sun a chance to dry out the side of this mountain." He was smiling, bouncing with every step all the way to the D4. I knew he was singing his own song in his head.

Rocky and Terry hurriedly collected the gear from the tent and piled it on the ground near the trailer without being told. The sun struggled to find a way through the hovering clouds while Carl readied the vehicles for the ride around Mt. Ryan. Around nine, a wind came up, tearing the clouds apart so sunlight could stream through a hole in the sky. The kittens scampered away after each other as Totem paced back and forth between the bulldozer and jeep.

For nearly an hour I searched for the kittens. I hollered for someone to help me from the bushes behind the tent, and again from the slope below camp, but no one came. I feared I would be unable to find the kittens by the time Carl was ready to leave. I was in a terrible frame of mind when I got back to the tent.

Carl had the jeep chained to the rear of the Cat. "We'll head for a small draw on the back side of the mountain which leads to a group of connecting ridges. If we make it up the draw without throwing a track we can follow the ridges until evening. Maybe we can make up some time."

Carl cranked up the D4. Suddenly Topsey and Holly bolted from a nearby clump of bushes. I was so relieved to see them. I bawled them out for running away and Topsey put up a good fight as I put them back in their box. I was curious about what had attracted the kittens, so I went to investigate.

Hidden among the bushes was a pile of large rocks, structured so precisely, one on top of the other, that I knew whoever took the time to carry the rocks also must have stacked them like this on purpose. I picked up a few rocks and threw them at the structure just in case something might be hiding nearby. That's when I discovered the entryway.

Overgrown weeds and bushes covered the hole but it was big enough for an animal the size of Totem to go through. I couldn't imagine what it was meant for, but in my mind, wolves were crouched inside. I mentioned to Carl the wolf den and my idea to explore it, but he dismissed my find with a "maybe so." Even if I wanted to return and inspect the place further, he said to get in the jeep, so I obeyed.

Carl angled the D4 on a slant and inched toward the base of the mountain. Everyone knew how dangerous this maneuver was. A great deal of moisture still clung beneath the moss where the sun couldn't shine. We moved around and down the mountain gradually, toward the draw (low ground between two ridges, often cut by a stream) on the other side of Mt. Ryan. The going was slow but steady.

I was concentrating on how the gravely slope we were ambling down joined the short green-carpeted draw below us when a sudden jolt whipped me backwards, throwing me sideways, hurling me into the door of the jeep. The rear of the bulldozer had swung wide. The jeep plunged for the valley below.

Mom gripped the steering wheel so tightly the knobby bones on her fists turned white. Before I could consider the consequences of the tow chain breaking and the jeep rolling down the mountain, Carl sank the blade of the D4 into the hillside.

"We're fine," Mom squeaked.

The boys looked back at us. Carl eased the bulldozer into reverse, moving slowly toward us.

I held my breath. I was scared to death we were going to slide down the mountain.

The D4 squealed. The jeep teetered to one side, and then the other. Without warning, the Cat slid from a giant rock hidden under the vegetation. The chain between the jeep and the D4 went slack and arched to the ground. Carl eased the D4 forward until the chain was stretched taut again, clear of the rock.

As we crawled on, down to the narrow draw, I looked behind us. I saw a deep scar carved in the side of the mountain in the shape of a half circle. We barely escaped a bad accident.

We crawled onto the top of the next ridge without difficulty and before us were nothing but gentle ridges. Even behind us, I saw a vast expanse of knobby hills, all above timberline. Carl opened the throttle wide. We sped along the ridge tops, tracks clacking a merry tune for the five of us. Mt. Ryan grew smaller and smaller until the ridges behind sank beneath the sky.

The relay system Carl worked out to get the vehicles to Mt. Ryan had worked according to plan. Though the plan had not run as smoothly or as quickly as Carl had hoped, the journey seemed easier now without the swamp buggy. The wooded valleys lay below us and we were on our way again.

We crossed the land bridges between the ridge tops without difficulty. Some of the steeper slopes took longer. Carl still did scouting, trail-building, searching for detours. After the near-tragedy, we all appreciated more deeply how he always made sure the route was safe.

I thought about the likelihood of someone living in the vast wooded lands below; a cabin could have been hidden easily within all those trees and no one would ever know. It was a scary thought because I wouldn't want to be walking by myself and run into a complete stranger.

We melted snow for water, stopped for lunch and short rest breaks, supper and sleep. Carl told plenty of jokes during our brief stops. The jeep stayed chained to the D4. I was not worried anymore about rolling down the mountainside.

Our caravan moved forward. Mom said little during the trek across the ridges, and I considered many things she might be thinking about. Mostly I wondered if she was having fun, but I didn't ask her. The whole world was in front of me. To keep my spirits up, I pretended Chena Hot Springs was just over the other side of the next ridge.

Through the windshield of the jeep, Rocky and Terry looked alert and loyal, like guards just before an attack. From positions on either side of Carl, they kept a lookout for bears, caribou, moose and every other wild animal they could imagine. When they got bored they turned around and made faces at me.

One morning I saw a black bear with three cubs. The mother bear circled in one spot the same way Totem does when he chases his tail. Then she nudged her triplets away from the noisy yellow creature invading her territory. Off they ran, the mama and her cubs, over the other side of the mountain and out of sight, like black balls, but rolling uphill. Carl explained later that echoes from the D4 bouncing between the ridges likely confused the sow so she couldn't quite make out which direction the strange noise was coming from.

The next day we descended into the narrow gorge of Frozenfoot Creek. It was early afternoon. Carl stopped the Cat on the small gravel bar. "Let's camp here tonight," he said, jumping to the ground.

I helped unload the gear without questioning why we had stopped, despite the fact that we had never set up camp this early in the day. Lately, there had been a lot of weird reasons for doing things, like getting kittens for a birthday present, Chuck coming to the family party, and Carl keeping the trip a secret. There had to be a reason this time. I just couldn't think of one.

The boys and I carried supplies to a densely wooded bank above the creek. Between two birch trees near the creek, Carl and the boys unfolded the tent. Mom set up the Coleman stove. I helped Mom, waiting for her to explain why we had stopped earlier than usual. Mom and I were still getting the kitchen set up when "the men" entered the tent.

"I'm going to search for the fishing poles," Carl said, reaching for a bucket. "Maybe we can catch a slew of grayling for supper." He left the tent with the bucket.

"We're going to the creek," Terry said as he and Rocky headed out of the tent after Carl. A short time later I followed the boys to the creek. I was barefoot and knee deep in creek water downstream from camp when I heard Mom yell, "Whose turn is it to get water?" She was standing outside the tent holding out a bucket.

"His turn," I yelled back, pointing at Terry.

"Terry's!" Rocky shouted, splashing creek water at Terry with one foot.

"Is not," snapped Terry, his face turning pink. "I got it last time. Besides, Carl already got some."

"Boys, get some water," Mom yelled.

Rocky chimed in. "You lost the game, remember? Loser has to get the next one. It's your turn."

"Yeah," I said, my hands on my hips, "you know what Carl said. And besides, he didn't get any water. He took the bucket to put fish in."

Terry's face turned bright red. He struggled to put his shoes on wet feet. "Just seeing if you remembered," he grumbled, as he stomped back to the tent, took the bucket from Mom and kicked rocks all the way back to the creek.

"Found the fishing poles in the bottom of the trailer," Carl announced. He positioned three collapsible metal fly rods on the gravel bar and then motioned for Rocky and me to join him.

I wanted a quick drink of water so I cupped my hands and drew some river water. "Ah! Better than Kool-Aid," I said to Rocky, wiping my mouth with the bottom of my shirt.

Terry marched by on his way back to the tent with a bucketful of water, glaring at me. "Kool-Aid's better," he said.

By that time, Carl had found three black and white mosquitoes in an assortment of dry flies he kept in a see-through tackle box with all his fly-fishing gear. He gave us one each.

"They're the best for catching grayling this time of year," he said, and proceeded to show us how to attach a fly to the clear leader line. The poles were rigged with thick orange fishing line and at least two feet of clear leader. "Poke the clear leader through the metal hook of the mosquito head. Then wrap the end of the leader line around three times, bring it back through the loop and pull tight."

We tried several times. It was difficult.

"You kids realize our food supply is just about gone, don't you?" Carl asked.

"Yeah, Mom told us no more snacking," Terry said, back from the water run.

"That's right," Carl stated. Now I felt a little nervous about fishing.

"She said we couldn't feed Totem snacks anymore, either," Rocky said.

"Your mom's right. We have to save it for ourselves. Totem and the cats have their own food," Carl said.

I'd seen Mom skimp on canned milk and eggs while we were stormed in on Mt. Ryan. She used water instead of milk and no eggs at all in the pancake mix. At supper she had opened one can of vegetables instead of two, but no one said anything.

"There's still some food in the old cellar of the Lodge," Carl said, "but we have to make sure we don't run out before we get there. We all have to help." The boys said they understood.

We poked our leaders into the heads of the mosquito flies as Carl told us how he'd purchased stock in Chena Hot Springs the year before, how there were a lot of stockholders, mostly businessmen from Fairbanks who had purchased the Springs in June of 1953. He said the stock was divided into shares that were printed on paper and all the stockholders plus their shares equaled a corporation. He said it was like a pie, where some had bigger slices than others.

His slice wasn't as big as some of the others, but he was hired to manage the Springs.

I wrapped the leader line around three times and pulled tightly. The line knotted securely against the fly's metal eye.

"Fish here awhile first," said Carl, "and try those two deep holes over there under the overhanging willows. Fish like big holes, to hide from us better."

Terry threw his line in first. "There's fish on the bottom! I can see 'em."

"Shh," Carl whispered. "You'll scare the fish away. They can hear you."

Sure enough, two fish shot across the bottom of the creek to the opposite bank. Again and again we threw our lines into the water and watched them drift over the ripples, hoping big fish would bite our mosquitoes. I tried casting farther but the fish still didn't bite. Soon Rocky moved to one of the deeper holes upstream. Terry walked downstream, casting as he walked.

Visions of catching a mess of fish excited the pioneer lady in me. I was determined the boys would not out-fish me so I remained near camp to try for one of the fish we'd seen, casting my line into the ripples, thinking about paper stock and pie slices and how we were running out of food.

We were close to the end of our trip. It didn't make sense to me that Carl should be so concerned about running out of food when there was food in the swamp buggy. All we had to do was walk back for it if we got that hungry. There had to be another reason why we stopped so early.

"Fish would have been nice," Mom said dishing up canned stew and camp bread with a smile, even though fish wasn't her favorite food and she disliked cooking it even less.

"We'll try again another time," Carl said, biting into the bread. Round, flat and salty, Mom had fried it till golden brown. It was Carl's favorite. The boys wouldn't try it.

On the gravel bar later that night, we roasted the last of the marshmallows to brown, gooey, puff-balls over a big campfire. When the firewood turned bright red and the gurgling of the creek seemed louder than during the day, Carl told us to watch the sky for Chuck's plane. He and Mom left for a walk along the creek.

It was then I realized we had stopped early in the day because Carl was concerned that Chuck might not find us. Rocky and Terry had gathered forked sticks among the willows a short distance up the creek for roasting marshmallows. Now they compared who had the stickiest stick, then the shortest stick. Boys were always comparing.

The fire burned down to tiny red coals before Mom and Carl returned to camp.

Chuck never came.

The comedians of the wilderness, camp robbers, flew into camp before breakfast next morning. Screeching, marching along the narrow bank of Frozenfoot Creek, over the rocks of the small gravel bar like ruthless pirates searching for a treasure, they poked between rocks with hooked beaks and scratched at the charred sticks from last night's campfire.

The scavengers squawked at each other and chased smaller birds away. They strutted across the rocks and gawked at the tent, jerking their heads from left to right while beady eyes peered at me with strange intensity. There were twelve of them, twelve like me. As soon as they stole all they could find, they flew away.

"A road has to be cut to the bare ridge above that high meadow," Carl said to Mom after breakfast. "Then I can tow the jeep out." He pointed to the high wooded bank on the other side of the creek. "It's the only way out. You kids find something else to do. A track might hit a rock and the D4 could slide backwards. Stay clear of the bulldozer."

Troubled by Carl's orders, I sat on the gravel bar near the tent, watching the bulldozer gnaw at the hillside across the creek until the sun was nearly overhead. The steel blade rolled boulders from its path and struggled to remove a large tree. Finally Carl jumped down to the ground and headed to the tree with an ax.

I could see it was going to be a long wait. I climbed the hill behind the tent to a small cliff overlooking camp. From there I had a perfect view of the path Carl was clearing, up a very steep bank. He was still chopping at the tree. I caught a brief glimpse of the boys, a short distance upstream, fly-fishing again.

The hacking of the ax boomed a final time and Carl dragged the felled tree to the side of the trail. He jumped back on the D4 and continued the struggle toward a meadow above the creek. From where I sat, the bulldozer looked like a toy.

I climbed higher. I dug some holes in the side of the hill with a sharp stick, hoping I would spook out an animal, but no luck. I threw rocks into the creek and watched them splash into the water before I heard them, I was so high up. Scrambling even higher, I found a rusty can nailed to a stump. Prying the lid back with the stick, I found several water-spotted papers stuffed inside the old can. A drawing on one of the papers had been partly torn away.

I sat near the stump and studied the faded markings. Whoever had placed the papers in the can could have been hunters. They could have wanted to build a cabin, but the drawings looked more like a map to me. The idea of finding a secret gold mine sent tingles down my spine and legs and into my shoes. I searched for a cave or a big hole, but found nothing. I was so excited I scurried down the hill to show everyone.

As soon as they returned from fishing, I showed my brothers what I found. "You could help me dig for it," I told them, waving the yellowed papers in their faces.

"That's just more of that surveyor stuff," Rocky said looking at the papers.

"Yeah, like Carl found on Mt. Ryan," Terry said.

Rocky laughed. "If it is a gold map, they wouldn't leave it where you could find it."

Chuck finally found the Wilsons camped on Frozenfoot Creek as they approached the end of their long journey. Chuck is shown here in the same Piper Super Cub which he eventually owned for 54 years.

"Yeah, they'd bury it. Wouldn't they Rocky?" Terry checked with the expert.

"Maybe."

"If it is a map to a gold strike and I find it without you, the gold is all mine!" I said. The boys chuckled as they walked on downstream.

Mom was slicing Spam into little sticks when I told her about my discovery. She said the drawings were probably land measurements. All through lunch I chattered about tracking down the gold mine, quietly hoping Carl would help me in my quest.

"Can't go with you right now, Gwennie. You and your mother need to start packing. It shouldn't be much longer before we're ready to leave."

We were still waiting for Carl to finish the road when the sun slid behind the trees on the hill across the creek. I had waited to return to the spot where I had found the rusty can, hoping Carl would still search the hillside with me before we left. Another hour passed and I was about to retrace my steps to the stump and start digging by myself when Carl clattered back across the creek with the bulldozer.

"Want to get out of this canyon and up that mountain before it gets late," he said. "Start loading the gear."

The D4 idled on the bank of Frozenfoot Creek as he inspected the chain between it and the jeep.

"It's not very far," I said. "Just a little ways from where the tent was. Please?"

"Not now," Carl said, pulling on the chain until it was tight.

"When you get through working on that?"

"Not now, Gwennie."

"Before we leave, could you walk up with me and just look?"

Carl motioned for Mom to get in the jeep. He hollered to the boys to get on the D4. I climbed into the jeep, shoved the papers underneath my seat and slammed the door. Mom slid the gearshift into neutral. The Caterpillar slowly crossed the creek, towing our jeep.

As we climbed the far bank toward a high slope above the grassy meadow, I sank into my seat and glared at Carl through the windshield. All I wanted was to go back. I knew if there were a mine up there, I wouldn't give up till I found it. Being twelve, though, I also knew there was probably nothing there. Carl would have searched for it, if there were. But now I would never know for sure. For the first time since the trip began I was not excited about moving on.

The D4 moaned as Carl steered up the uneven pathway he had cut on the hillside that morning. The path narrowed and the Cat aimed for the clouds, the boys gripping the back of Carl's seat as they faced the sky.

I could see a clear view of the creek through Mom's window. The bulldozer sputtered. There had to be only inches of road, just a small strip of earth between the track of the D4 and the edge of the cliff. I checked again through Mom's window. My view of the creek looked fuzzy, as queasiness stuck to the sides of my stomach. It was a long drop to the water.

The muscles between my shoulders stung as I tightened my grip on the seat.

Suddenly, there was a piercing ring. Steel clanged against steel. The jeep lunged backwards.

The jolt threw me back onto the dusty roof of the cab. I grabbed the dashboard with my left hand and held on to the rim of the open door window with the other. The jeep plunged again.

Mom slammed her foot on the brakes. The pedal hit the floor with a thud. She pumped the brake pedal again and again.

Thud, thud, thud.

Backwards down the hill we rolled, the bulldozer we were following shrinking from view.

"I can't stop the jeep!" Mom yelled. She punched the brake again. She pulled the emergency brake. "Oh, good Lord! The brakes don't work!" she yelled.

The churning in my stomach filled my eyes with tears, and a fear bigger than I had ever known swelled inside me as I pictured the jeep with Mom and me inside, toppling over the bank.

Thud, thud, thud, thud.

The jeep swerved to the side and Mom yanked the steering wheel the other way.

We could not see the D4. The trailer we were pulling jerked left, then right. I knew one wrong turn would send us crashing into the creek.

Thud, thud, thud.

The trailer rammed the side of the hill. The jeep scraped the rocky embankment. Everything went into slow motion. The jeep and trailer aimed straight for the edge of the cliff. My kittens, upside down on the floor behind my seat, yowled. Mom swung the wheel to the right. We turned sharply and hit a tree. A limb plunged through my open window, bent the metal bar across the top of the glass and shattered the windshield. The branch drug across my hand and gouged my cheek.

The jeep rolled backward. My face throbbed. Blood covered my fingers. My hand and face stung. I wanted to cry.

Smacking rocks, hitting ruts, the jeep slid down the narrow path of the hill till we rolled to a stop in the middle of Frozenfoot Creek. As quickly as the chain between the bulldozer and jeep had snapped and metals clashed, the rush of fear suddenly ended. How Mom kept the trailer from jackknifing was a miracle!

All I could hear was the rush of water beating against the tires.

My legs shook as I struggled from the jeep and stepped into the brisk creek water. Keeping the tears inside had been a struggle all the way down the mountainside as Carl's words echoed in my head: "Wilsons are strong. Wilsons don't cry!"

Mom and I waded through the icy current toward the bank, helping each other over slippery rocks and up the bank. Exhausted and sick from terror, I sank down onto the weeds. Mom sat down too, looking pale.

The horror of falling kept replaying in my mind as I sat on the bank next to Mom. My eyes were full of moisture. I was afraid the tears would spill this time, run all over my face. I kept hearing "Wilsons don't cry. Crying is a sign of weakness, and no one in this family is weak."

No one in this family ever cries, I thought. The urge to cry ached in my throat. *I am strong,* I told myself. *I am strong. What if I can't keep from crying?* I held back the tears. I was a Wilson!

"Belle," Carl called. "You all right?" The boys, eyes big as saucers, were close on Carl's heels as the three fellows ran down the hill toward us. I could tell Carl was mad, the way he stopped and glared at Mom.

"Why didn't you use the brakes?"

I had never seen him furious with Mom. Not even when he bawled out the boys and me for playing with matches last winter was he this angry. It wasn't her fault. The brakes didn't work.

"She *did* use the brakes," I muttered.

My face hurt to speak. He thought we went over the side. The pain in my cheek throbbed. It hurt to touch, even though the bleeding had stopped. My hand stung.

Images of the fall continued flashing in my head, switching to what could have happened, the jeep and trailer plunging over the bank, crashing into the creek, flipping in the air and landing upside down, our bodies crushed beneath the jeep, pinned under the water.

"Belle!" Carl yelled again. "Why didn't you use the brakes?"

He stood with his hands on his hips, his eyes darting back and forth from Mom to me. Rocky and Terry didn't move from their spot on the other side of Mom.

I couldn't stop my legs from shaking. Now even my arms, knees and back were shaking. I felt cold. Rocky and Terry were silent, staring at Mom.

"I did, Carl, but nothing happened," Mom said quietly, her face expressionless. "They didn't work, Carl. The brakes don't work."

Mom and I sat on the graded dirt. She wiped my face with a fresh Kleenex she took from inside the cuff of her shirtsleeve. "I think your face will be okay," she said to me. "Just a bad scratch."

After awhile everyone calmed down. Carl waded the creek to check on Topsey and Holly. He left them in the jeep. *I guess they went to sleep*, I thought. They were quiet, anyway.

"There's not many moms as good-lookin' as your mom, who could drive that jeep backwards into a creek," he said, grinning nervously. I could tell that seeing us fall had shaken him up.

Rocky was trying to laugh, but kept poking the palm of his left hand with his right pointer, like he always did when he got into trouble. "We thought you fell in the creek," he said to Mom, sheepishly.

Carl joked again about flying down the mountain backwards.

"Well, I guess we did do that, sort of," Mom said just above a whisper. She tugged off her wet shoes and socks. Terry, eyes down, bobbed his head up and down, agreeing with everything, I guess. He had dug a small hole in the dirt with the heel of his right boot, not knowing what else to do.

Once I could walk without shaking, I skimmed rocks across the creek with Rocky and Terry to see whose rock could skip the most times. Carl stood at the bank a long while, looking at the jeep with Mom near his side. After a time he took the long walk up the hill to the bulldozer, alone. Mom sat by the creek, staring at the water.

This time around, Carl secured the jeep to the rear of the Cat with three chains. "Chances of three breaking at the same time are slim."

We started up the side of the mountain again. I was sure we'd know if a chain broke, but that idea didn't help me feel any better. I gripped my seat with both hands as fears from before swelled inside me. *It was more fun in the old days*, I thought, *long skirts and horses instead of jeans, jeeps, and bulldozers.*

At the top of the mountain, under an early evening sky, our steel caravan lumbered along the ridge toward yet another ridge. Carl opened the throttle wider. Whooping and hollering, we made some progress before the chill of evening settled in around us. The jeep bumped and Totem loped, his tongue flopping out the side of his mouth in time to the rhythm of the steel tracks.

I reached under my seat for the faded yellow papers to the hidden gold mine and flung them out the window. *Goodbye, Frozenfoot Creek,* I thought. *You can keep your gold.*

Chapter 11

Headwinds

We arrived at the end of another chain of ridges. Carl said we had now traveled over more mountains than we had left to go. Across the valley below us was the only way to get to the next group of ridges.

Carl set out downhill toward the narrow wooded valley to scout for a route, with Rocky scampering behind. The woods all looked the same to me. The bald, gray-blue mountains rolled on ahead as far as I could see. Though the goal Carl had set for our family still waited in the distance, the fun of camping had dulled as much for me as for the boys. They were beginning to miss town activities and their friends. I was getting tired of washing dishes while the boys got to play and Mom said more than once she wished she could have a bath and eat her dinner from a table for a change. Carl tried to keep everyone's spirits high but it was obvious to me he was running out of jokes. He had been telling some of them over again.

"Don't forget to save some of that snow for water, Terry," Mom called.

"Okay," Terry yelled back. He made a beeline for the backside of the ridge.

"Just a little catnap, Gwennie," Mom said, as she stretched out on the ground in the shade of the D4. Carl's gun was on the ground near her head. Carl had never left the gun with Mom before, not that I could remember. Maybe he forgot it this time. Then, maybe he had a good reason for leaving it behind. I didn't have an answer to any of my questions so I decided it didn't matter.

I watched Carl and Rocky disappear into the timber a quarter of the way down the mountain. It would be a long wait. Since I was going to have to spend the time by myself I decided to look for odd rocks and ugly bugs. I walked the ridge, away from the parked vehicles cooling in the wind.

I had walked only a short distance when I heard a bird call. I couldn't see the bird but the haunting two-note tune kept in perfect time with the wind's whistle. I kept walking, looking for the bird. A week into our trek, I had learned the wind made high-pitched whistles, or low-keyed whistles, depending on the height of the mountain. Carl said when the wind blew through the different sized rock crevices the quality of the sound changed.

I continued along the top of the slope hoping to spot the little bird again and listening to the wind whistling. After a time I heard the bird call out agin, intense and nearby. The urgency of the call brought me to a standstill.

Without blinking an eye, I scanned the gully below me. I saw a large pile of black rocks covered with swirling patches of gray mountain moss near the floor of the gully. The rocks twisted into a magnificent sculpture, reaching for the sky. I heard the eerie call twice more. I examined every fragment of ground, every scrubby bush, and every rock, but nothing moved.

If the bird called again I was sure I could find it. I stepped farther down the slope, closer to the bottom of the gully and squatted down, leaning in against the rocky hillside. The bird called out again.

Perched on a jagged edge of one of the black rocks near the center of the massive nature-piled monument, I saw a small, brown bird. I had imagined a much larger bird from the strength of its call. I didn't know the name of the bird; I had never seen one like it before. I leaned onto the slope and waited.

The rock formations below reminded me of a lesson we had in school about when the earth was in a terrible era of turmoil and change. Mrs. Parent explained to us there had been an endless upheaval of hot volcanic rock, which spread over the surface of many continents. There were pictures in my science book of the remains of those angrier ages. The rocks in the gully looked just like the pictures in my book, of cooled-off lava. This bird had made the leftover lava into a safe haven for her chicks.

It wasn't long before the bird hopped to a higher rock, then onto another rock, and yet another, higher and higher along the jagged points. Swifter than the wind blew across my face, the bird swept in front of me and landed a few feet above, on a large weathered stone. Rigid and alert, the bird repeated the two-note call.

I followed the bird to the top of the ridge. "Don't be scared, little fellow. I won't hurt you. Please don't be scared. I'm not going to bother your babies."

The bird flew to the other side.

"Now, why did you do that? You can't leave your babies alone. You just can't." I scrambled to the top of the slope, but the bird was gone. I sat down on a flat rock and stared at the mountains. Gray haze clouded the miles ahead. Behind me, the Caterpillar was a blur of yellow.

"One of these days," I said aloud, "we'll be on top of one of those slopes over there and Carl will shout, 'There's Chena Hot Springs... down there in that valley!'"

I continued walking the ridge, the mountain moss cracking beneath the rubber soles of my dirty sneakers, drinking in the aroma of sun-baked pine needles. I heard Terry yell as he played. The temperatures cooled and the wind gusts scraped the barren ridge, sweeping moss and twigs across my path. A few wind-scattered seeds had managed to take root on the yellow-brown slope. Now their delicate blooms seemed to smile at me.

I heard Terry yell again. The bird called, its haunting melody more intense.

"You must be here! Why are you hiding from me?"

I walked farther and still, the wind carried Terry's fake war cries along the ridge. He'd play until Carl and Rocky returned if he didn't run out of snowballs. I hoped he'd remember to leave a clean patch of snow for water.

The vehicles were only smudges in the distance now, and no sign of Carl and Rocky's return. I drew designs on the boulders with a jagged piece of white stone, walked over to sit in the scratchy moss and watched the wind drag fluffy clouds across the sky.

As I watched, the biggest cloud changed into an old man with a long white beard and cane, then he turned into a big dog with floppy ears and a long tail. The longer I watched, the more shapes I saw. Sailboats raced, cars trundled along on bumpy roads, and an ugly monster chased smaller monsters into a beautiful castle with many high towers. A few moments later, the castle crumbled apart across the sky and the wind turned the towers into scoops of ice cream with whipped cream.

I scrambled to my feet and looked back to survey our temporary camp. The D4's bright yellow color was gone. The jeep looked fuzzy. I had walked much farther than I realized, so I headed back, now craving graham crackers and ice cream, as I marched along the slope like a soldier on guard, pacing the catwalk of the fort. Up ahead, I saw Terry standing at the top of the rise, behind the vehicles. Terry's yelling turned to screams as he pointed to the valley on the other side of the mountain, his hair vivid white.

Thinking it was Carl and Rocky coming back, I ran toward the vehicles with hopes of leaving soon. I passed the vehicles and headed for Mom, who was standing on the ridge overlooking the valley. Her hands were to her forehead, shielding the sun. She stooped down and grabbed hold of Carl's gun. Mom took aim.

Terry's high-pitched voice wailed again: "Mom! Mom! A bear! A bear's chasing Carl and Rocky!"

I stood at Mom's side, terror squeezing my insides until I was numb. Carl and Rocky were running up toward us from the bottom of the valley with Totem in the lead. On their heels loped a big, black bear.

Carl and Rocky hollered garbled words over their shoulders at the bear. Carl grabbed rocks and hurled them backwards. Shiny black fur rolled and rippled.

Mom lowered the gun. She raised the gun again, peering through the rifle site, dropped her aim a few inches, looked again into the valley, and again raised the gun to take aim.

A cry of sorrow and fear swirled within me, making my stomach churn. The beast's strides, on huge, padded paws, were almost graceful, reminding me of the little bird that flew away from me, so programmed to fight or flee.

The mounds of black fur grew larger as the bear advanced up the mountain.

Where could we go if the bear came all the way to the top? I glanced at Terry. Terry was silent. His nose wrinkled up as he tried not to cry.

Why didn't Mom shoot? What was she waiting for? Mom set the gun down on the ground and started boring a hole into the hard dirt near her shoes with the tip of the gun's barrel. What was she doing? What were we going to do?

Suddenly the bear halted. He flopped back on his rear end, as though considering a new thought. The wind grew silent. The bear rose, stood for a moment on his hind legs, scanning the hillside above him, at Carl and Rocky nearing the top of the slope, at Terry wiping back the tears, and at me and Mom, with the shotgun poked into the ground like a crutch. The bear plopped down on all fours, turned and ran back toward the treeline.

"Did you see that bear?" Carl called, panting as he came to a halt at the top of the ridge. His face was streaked with wet dirt, his eyes dancing. "Thought I was going to have to wrestle him," he huffed.

Rocky's big smile looked out of place on his pasty white face. Mom was unearthing more dirt and pebbles beside her shoe with the tip of the gun. It wasn't like her to stand down. She was the one who always told me things would be okay, who worked so hard to make things okay. She should have shot the bear.

"It isn't funny. What if I had missed the bear and hit one of you?" she said, shaking away the awful thought.

Totem raced back down the slope and disappeared into the timberline.

Carl put his arms around Mom. "You boys better go call Totem," Carl said. "That bear's long gone by now but don't go too far down that hill." He took the gun from Mom and leaned it against the jeep, then sat down on the ground with Mom. I squatted down beside Carl.

"I thought the bear was coming all the way up here," I whispered.

"And so did I, for awhile," Carl said. "She has cubs hidden down there in the brush somewhere and I guess she thought we were going to harm them. I'm sure that's the same bear I saw ambling down a ridge shortly before we stopped."

"You guys did look funny, high-tailing it up the mountain with a bear after your fannies," Mom said, her words still shaky.

From the ridge, we could still see the boys. Carl never took his eyes off of them. After twenty minutes they returned with Totem. Terry took a bucket to melt snow. I called Topsey and Holly and put them in their box.

"Rocky and I found a good way off this mountain," Carl said, setting the shotgun next to his seat on the bulldozer, after double-checking the chamber. "We'll make camp at the bottom tonight. There's a creek down there. In the morning we'll climb the next mountain."

No one said anything more about the bear. Totem stayed in the shade of the jeep and panted until the vehicles were ready for departure. When Carl pulled himself up on the D4, the boys took their usual places next to him, while Mom and I climbed into the jeep. Carl gave the starter cord a hefty yank and Totem raced ahead of the bulldozer as we descended into the valley.

Maybe it was the hollering, or the rocks spinning within inches of the bear's face, or the scent of humans, but whatever had changed the bear's mind, nobody cared. We were lucky. And I wasn't hungry anymore. From the jeep, I wondered how Rocky was doing. He was still grinning, but now his face had returned to its normal shade of pink.

We wound alongside the slope, making switchbacks all the way to the bottom of the valley. I caught sight of the little bird from the corner of my eye just before we got to the timberline. It flew alongside us, rested on a rock for a few seconds, then flitted into the trees and was gone.

I felt sorry for the bird and the bear, having to deal with us humans crossing through their homes and playgrounds; to them we were the enemy. For us, there was no other way to get to the Hot Springs. It was simple to me. In this desolate country, we couldn't begin to get along with each other when we looked with doubt at others' intentions. They were the enemy because we were the enemy. You can't explain such complicated lessons to a bear, even a clever one.

We made camp that evening beside Olympia Creek. Rocky and Terry had piled wood on the gravel bar and Carl said he was going to make a big fire. The boys rushed off to collect more wood.

"Do you know where George built his cabin, Carl?" Mom asked, poking a long stick into the fire. Sparks jumped, logs popped and crackled, and the sun slipped down the backside of the hill. The warmth from the fire felt good.

"Near Spring Creek, I think, downstream from the Swans' bathhouse, but on the opposite side of the creek. His first cabin burned down. The second one was built near the Lodge. He began to build a lot of smaller cabins, too. So did other people."

"On his land?" I asked.

"After George homesteaded the land he made a trip to town that fall for supplies. He met a young man named Charley who lived in Graehl, across the river from town," Carl said.

"The same Charley who walked in with George the first time?" I asked.

"No," Carl said, watching the sky, "a different Charley. His name was Charley Boyer. Charley was from Illinois, twenty-three years old with no experience in trapping...a Cheechako. George said he'd help Charley hunt and run a trapline and Charley could have half of what they caught if he'd help George at the homestead."

Carl rose and studied the sky. I heard the drone of an airplane.

"Maybe that's Chuck," Carl said, standing up.

He walked over to the water's edge. Mom and I followed. Just above the trees on the far side of the valley, I spotted it, a tiny dot growing bigger and bigger with every thump of my heart.

"He's following the creek," Carl said, walking to the water's edge.

"We're over here!" Terry yelled, waving his arms.

"Hey, down here!" Rocky hollered.

Chuck's Super Cub zoomed right over our heads. The boys danced over the rocks like puppets, arms flopping. Chuck continued up the creek, circled wide and headed back. He passed over our camp twice, tipping the wings to the right and to the left to say hello. We laughed, glad to greet our friend and show him we were still alive and kicking. He circled the camp once more then flew off south, toward Fairbanks. We stood perched on the rocks, watching Chuck's yellow plane slip away from us, disappearing into the horizon.

Mom and Carl started for the tent. "Bedtime, boys. Got to get up early," Carl called. "I'll finish that story."

"What's a Cheechako?" Terry asked. The boys darted into the tent, ready for stories.

I stayed at the creek, even though the hum of Chuck's plane had faded. We had been left alone, completely alone. I stood on the river rocks for I don't know how long, listening to the creek babble its song of contentment. The sun had set, but the summer sky was light, almost bright, and clear of clouds.

I wondered how I could feel lonely when Mom, Carl and the boys were chatting just a few steps away.

CHAPTER 12

Winter of 1908

———

"I was to have half of what we could catch trapping and hunting.
We went up the river to the North Fork, then up the
North Fork to the hot springs."
– Charles L. Boyer

George Wilson and Charley Boyer left Fairbanks on September 10, 1908 with a boat full of provisions and a gunny sack full of traps. Unbeknownst to George, while he was in town filing on his homestead and stocking up on supplies, Eugene Norton and William Ormsby were heading north on the Chena River from Fairbanks.

Two weeks later when George and Charley arrived at the homestead, they found Norton and Ormsby had been bathing daily and had set up a camp near the Swans' old bathhouse on George's property. George informed the men he had homesteaded the land but he didn't mind if they bathed until they were ready to leave.

George and Charley began cutting logs. George had already built a small cache for vegetables that spring and by the second week of October, they had built a one-room log cabin on Spring Creek. They left to hunt and clear a trapline and to put up two small line cabins so they could extend their range. There was very little hunting at that time of year because the annual caribou migration had not come through yet. When they returned to the homestead, George continued improving the inside of his cabin. When it was time to check the traps, Charley went alone. He was gone for six weeks. Near the end of November, George and Charley returned to Fairbanks to restock their supplies.

November skies turned darker and stayed that way most of the day because the sun had began its seasonal hibernation. Temperatures dropped to bitter cold. Often the moon glowed so bright on the snow-covered landscape that nights were brighter than days.

Late November 1908, three men prepared for a journey to the Hot Springs by dogsled on the Upper Chena River. Two teams of dogs left Fairbanks pulling three men and two heavy sleds. Traveling northeast of town through the snow-covered spruce trees, they hugged the flat river bottom of the frozen Big Chena River. Beyond this party of three men, the icy wilderness stretched out endlessly. The dogs' heavy panting, along with the squeaking of the handmade sleds and the hiss of the sled runners played off each other, a unique kind of wilderness music, as the teams broke trail toward Monument Creek Valley and the Hot Springs.

Fred A. Douse, James Leonard Heacock and Clarence D. McCauley had packed their sleds with stoves, food supplies and other provisions. McCauley was along for recreation. Heacock and Douse wanted to soak in the mineral water.

"When we left here," McCauley later said in a deposition, "I was in good health and went for no other reason than to help the boys....On the way up, there were about two days I had to haul Leonard Heacock and, probably a day in all, I had to haul Douse. They were unable to walk." (McCauley testimony, p.16)

McCauley, a truck farmer and a carpenter, was a native-born U.S. citizen who had lived in Fairbanks since February, 1903, near 8th and Noble. James L. "Lennie" Heacock was only 14 years old in September 1904, when his family moved from the warmth of Arizona to a home in Fairbanks on 5th Street, between Wickersham and Cowles. (Heacock testimony) Suffering intense pain from rheumatism (known today as rheumatoid arthritis), Douse had not been able to work. He was a chicken rancher by trade. Just the year before, he had stood proudly with his colleagues for a picture in front of the Fairbanks Fire Department, but the extreme cold took its toll on his joints.

George's homestead in 1908 after he leased the property to the Beams. The hotel is on the left and the bunk house on the right. Numerous spruce tree stumps remain in the foreground. *(Courtesy National Archives.)*

At first, Douse was reluctant to leave his wife behind in Fairbanks. She was sick in bed at their home on 8th and Cowles. But Douse, persuaded by his friends to try the waters of the Hot Springs for his debilitating condition, decided to make the trip. The sled dogs hauled him supine, for the weeklong trip to the Hot Springs. (Douse statement) When they arrived in the early part of December, the cabin built by Wilson and Boyer was unlocked. Inside, the three men found George's clothes, a few cooking utensils, a stove, and very little food but a comfortable bed for Douse.

"Mr. Wilson was away at the time. The cabin was open, and I was sick and I had to have some place to go to," Douse testified in 1913. "After I got well enough, I did the cooking for the boys."

In 1906, the Swans and Van Curler built out the bathhouse located over the largest hot spring. Still, it was only about eight feet by nine feet with a lean-to, or sweat room, about twelve feet square. The men decided they wanted more room, so McCauley began building an addition onto the east side of the Swan bathhouse for their own quarters. Douse and Heacock took baths in the hot water and drank both hot and cold mineralized water daily.

"We stayed in George Wilson's cabin while we built the addition which we afterwards lived in," Heacock said. "A man by the name of Raber, Mrs. I. B., and Wilson's brother were also at the hot springs."

In the meantime, John, "Jack" Sullivan and others had arrived. Sullivan was from Ester Creek and claimed to have been among the first hundred men in the Fairbanks area. "I had a little rheumatism in my hand, but was feeling pretty good and made the journey to the springs for just a trip," said Sullivan. (Sullivan testimony, p. 55)

By then, Douse, McCauley and Heacock had finished the addition onto the small sweat room. They put canvas bunks and a stove inside. Mr. Raber was living in the sweat room when Louis Behl, a miner, and his partner, Henry Smith, arrived at the Hot Springs. Behl had come to the United States from Germany about 1886. He had lived in Skagway, Alaska, since the winter of 1897-1898, but moved to the Fairbanks Mining District in October of 1904. Behl suffered from rheumatism and recently had been mining on Bedrock Bar on the Middle Fork. Hoping to rest and recuperate, he came to the Hot Springs with permission from Aaron Van Curler to use the Swan bathhouse. (Behl testimony) Smith and Behl also began to build a cabin, living in a tent until it was finished.

"At least I helped," Behl said. "I was pretty well knocked out with rheumatism." (Behl testimony)

The thirteen-foot-square cabin, on the right bank of the creek, was built to accommodate the visitors on future trips to the Hot Springs. They equipped the cabin with a stove, two blankets, a few towels and a cook outfit, finishing the work around December 14th. The two men proceeded to soak in the bathhouse. (Behl testimony)

Sullivan, Carey Richards and C.D. McCauley began to build a second cabin, twelve feet square, on the right bank of the creek. The site they chose was about sixty feet above the Swans' bathhouse, about 12 feet back from the creek, complete with a floor, a door and windows.

"Well, we never used it. We just built—put up the walls, chinked it with moss, and I think we cut four or five logs out of the doorway for a door and started the saw into one log in two places for a window," Sullivan said.

But before the cabin was completed, George Wilson and Charlie Boyer returned to the valley. George found his homestead an industrious settlement: people staking tents, building cabins, felling trees, reclining in the baths. This was his home! Didn't these men know he had claimed this land for a homestead?

He would tell them. He would also need to talk to them about cutting timber on his land. Taking baths in the healing water was one thing, but cutting timber was quite another. George had conscientiously complied with the regulations for homesteading. These "adverse possessors" would have to acknowledge his legal rights.

George approached the men. He informed McCauley and the others that he had homesteaded the land. He told them if they wanted to build cabins, they would have to go off his land to get the timber. (McCauley statement)

"I crossed over the line to get the material," McCauley said, "off his homestead, at the foot of the hill on the west side." (McCauley testimony)

George's staunch claim of ownership offended McCauley and the others. They felt it was unfair that this "Canadian," as they referred to him, had a right to own a natural hot springs, especially such a beneficial one.

> *"I wanted to use some moss for this cabin, but he told me about where to go to get it, as he was going to use the moss on his property. We mossed it good, and put a roof on it. Then we built a big fire the night before we left there, in the middle of it, so as to dry it out as much as possible...so the next comer might find it more comfortable."* (Sullivan testimony)

Sullivan, McCauley and the rest of the squatters prepared to leave. After the first week of soaking and drinking the waters of the hot springs, Douse and Heacock had improved considerably! Now they were walking.

The visitors were convinced that a hot springs with such wonderful healing powers, as these appeared to have, should be open for the use of the general public. "In three weeks' time they were ready to come home," said McCauley. "That is what it (the mineralized water) did for those two." (McCauley testimony)

Disregarding George's claim, the men placed a sign over the door of each cabin they had built, before leaving for Fairbanks. Douse's sign read: "For Use by the Public, When Not Occupied by the Owners." (McCauley and Douse statements, Sullivan testimony) After they signed their names on the notice and packed up their dogsleds, they mushed onto the trail and headed southwest across the Tanana Valley. According to later testimony, Wilson tore their buildings down as soon as the men left.

When McCauley returned to Fairbanks that December, there were close to fifteen people who had traveled from Fairbanks now encamped on George's homestead. McCauley realized he hadn't paid George Wilson anything for using the hot springs, but neither had George asked him to.

George hadn't denied anyone the use of the natural baths. But he couldn't let them cut the trees on his land for fuel or for house logs. It just wasn't right. He had always been very careful and he cautioned the others to be careful, not to let fire get out among the timber.

"Everything seemed to be free," Louis Behl said. "Everything was free in the bathhouse. Everybody, it seems like, helped themselves." (Behl testimony)

But, McCauley was upset by the encounter with Wilson. On the way back to town Douse was now strong enough to mush the dogs all the way to Fairbanks. The men discussed the matter and agreed the hot waters on the land the Canadian was homesteading should never be allowed to be owned by one individual, (McCauley statement), let alone an immigrant.

Towards the end of December, McCauley and the others watched George, who "...began cutting just as we were leaving there," McCauley said. "He cut all the large timber on the bank." (McCauley testimony, p. 20)

With Charley away, George's progress in clearing the land was slow. Every few weeks, Charley needed to leave camp to check the trapline. Once the trees were felled, the soil needed cultivation. Getting the ground ready for planting by the spring was expensive and time-consuming.

The trapping season would end when spring came. Charley would then need to collect all the traps, clean and repair any damaged ones, hang them up for next winter and be ready for beaver trapping down on the main river by April. Right now trapping was their only source of income. (Even today, the North Fork is a prime area for marten [sable] which, at that time, sold for about $20 each, or $565 in today's dollars.) It is not known how long this trapping arrangement lasted, but the 1910 US Census shows Charles L. Boyer, age 27, as a member of the George Wilson Household. Charley's time was being well spent on the trapline, and critical to Wilson's mission! If George were to remain on the land, he couldn't let anything—weather, squatters, or discouragement—delay him. He knew he couldn't do all the work alone, so he employed whoever came along for a time, mostly trading out rent.

Behl stayed at the Hot Springs until the middle of January, 1909. "Mr. Wilson was cutting logs for his big bathhouse when I was there." (Behl testimony) He ignored Wilson's homestead claim just as McCauley had. Before leaving for Fairbanks, Behl hung a sign on the door of the cabin he and Smith had built. In big letters, he wrote that the cabin was for "Smith, Behl and the Public" as though that would show George Wilson how things worked in these parts.

As Smith and Behl pulled away from the Hot Springs, three other men arrived, then proceeded to unload their supplies into their cabin (Behl Testimony), with barely enough time to read the new sign on the door.

George set his jaw and hacked away another spruce.

CHAPTER 13

Arrival

Tuesday, June 1, 1954

After two drawn-out days of unending ridges following the night of Chuck's overflight, the tires of the jeep and trailer rolled onto a barren mountaintop. The D4 jerked to a stop, its steel blade hitting the ground with a thud.

Carl shut the engine off and jumped down, waving at Mom and me to get out of the jeep. The boys peered over the nose of the D4.

Carl stood straight, looking taller than usual against the vastness of the sky. Before I had time to wonder, he shouted with an eagerness I hadn't heard in days.

"There it is!" he shouted, glancing at us, grinning broadly. "There's Chena Hot Springs!"

I threw open the jeep door and jumped to the rocky ground, savoring the words I'd waited so long to hear. My thoughts came alive: the swimming pool, hot baths, ancient cabins, my new bedroom, the kitchen, dining room. Scenes I'd carried since Faith Creek and Steese Highway now snapped in my mind, one by one, like Carl's slides. I ran to the top of the ridge, Mom close behind.

My eyes trailed 2500 feet down the thickly wooded ridge, across a long, wide valley. My stomach sank, for all I saw was more mountains, no buildings, and nothing resembling steam.

Was he joking? He wouldn't. Not about this.

I turned to question Carl's announcement just as something on the floor of the valley caught my eye. Faint lines of an old trail wound along the valley floor to the river.

"George's old trail!" I screamed.

Carl nodded, grin still in place.

"Yay! Wait, where's the steam?" Terry asked, scratching his head, hopping from one foot to the other. The boys nearly tripped each other, scrambling from the D4. They ran to the ledge and stood beside us.

"Not far, now!" Carl went on. "We've got four weeks to clean the place up. We'll haul the old junk away, fix up the dining room. It'll be a snap. Belle, you and Gwennie can make curtains. Look at that. We're almost there!" Across the valley, sunlight glittered on the river winding through spruce trees and wide-open grassy spaces until the river and the old trail came together. There the trail disappeared into the mountains on the other side of the valley.

"It's just behind that small ridge," Carl went on.

"Where?" asked Rocky. "I don't see it."

"I don't see it, either," Terry said.

"Behind the ridge that runs down to the river." Carl pointed to his left, now standing on the D4 and traced the ridge, making an outline in the air with a sweep of his arm.

"Monument Creek Valley!" he shouted. "See it? When we get to the river we're only about a mile from the Hot Springs." He rested his hands on his hips and sighed.

"I don't see anything," Rocky grumbled, studying the valley, his hands on his hips like Carl.

"You can't see the Hot Springs yet," I said, shaking my head. "Don't you know anything? It's behind that big ridge." I searched for the opening Carl had pointed to. I thought it must be where the trail went behind the ridge, but not wanting to admit I didn't know, I kept quiet.

Somewhere in the distance I heard a bird call. A warm breeze fluttered across my face and the realization that we would reach the

Hot Springs that evening almost made me cry. The view of those wooded ridges sliding onto the valley floor was a magnificent scene. We weren't going to cross any more mountains. At that moment I was more excited than when I found the kittens. I wanted to yell.

Carl jumped from the D4. "Now, you guys look close—down near the river," he said, putting his hands on the boys' shoulders. "On the left is a small opening in the hills. We go through the opening for a mile or so, then into a small valley. See it?"

"Oh, yeah," Rocky said, nodding and pointing. "Over there."

"Yeah. I see it, too," Terry said.

"I'm going swimming when we get there. Are you, Terry?" I knew Rocky hadn't seen it; he'd pointed in the wrong direction.

Mom looked relieved, staring at the valley. Carl put his arm around her. There our family stood, silent on the edge of the big hill in this wilderness, far from the busyness of Fairbanks. This valley was the last hurdle, before reaching our goal.

"Belle, anything to nibble on when we get back?" Carl asked. Mom nodded sure. "I'm going to walk down the slope. Check for a route." Mom looked happier than she had since leaving Faith Creek.

"How much longer?" I asked. "Are we going to get there tonight? How long will it take? Are we sleeping in the old lodge tonight? Will we...."

Carl chuckled. "Yes!" he said, winking. "We'll be there tonight if..." He paused and scanned the mountain, "...if everything goes smoothly."

Shoulders back, head high, chin in that familiar straight-forward position, Carl turned and marched down the mountain toward the valley. He looked back for Rocky and Terry. "You boys coming?" They loped after him.

This wait won't be long, I thought, watching them cross the side of the mountain through tall brush. The boys' heads sank from sight. I let the kittens out of their box to run.

"Gwennie, make some Kool-Aid," Mom said, opening the food box. "Gosh, there's only one pack of Kool-Aid left. Hope they aren't too thirsty."

Mom said we'd get water soon, brushing away a fly from the soda crackers she'd set on the hood of the jeep. "Make what's left. Shoo! Get away, nasty fly!"

It was the longest wait of the trip; time probably dragged on because we were practically done with the trip. Mom spread peanut butter on crackers and talked about the old stable, and how many horses George might have had. She explained how the generator made electricity so we could use the toilets in the Lodge, and how big the swimming pool was. Mostly she talked about the work ahead of us. The job sounded enormous: washing dishes, cleaning cabins, washing linens, mopping floors. I dumped the last packet of punch into the metal pitcher. Strawberry flavor smelled good. I added the sugar and water.

"Now all the water's gone," I said.

"Then they'll just have to wait until we get to the river."

Mom stared out over the valley, probably longing for a nice hot bath and a second cup of coffee from a china cup—maybe even clean sheets. The last two weeks would soon be a memory.

An hour later Carl and the boys returned.

"It's steep," Carl reported, gulping down a cup of Kool-Aid. "I'm going to have to angle a road part way down this slope." He drank two more cups and poured a fourth. Munching on cracker sandwiches made with the last of the peanut butter, Carl leaned against the jeep, while the boys made bets about how long Carl would take to make this trail. Everything was a contest for them.

There was only a half cup of Kool-Aid left in the pitcher when I went to fill my cup. I walked down the slope and sat on a rock. Why were the boys always first?

"Shouldn't take long," I heard Carl say.

I'm always last. I'm the one who's going to have to wait until we get to the river for water. It's not fair.

As the mountain air cooled, we began the descent down the mountain, on a switchback roadway that angled toward the treeline. Once again the vehicles crept over freshly dug earth we had watched

Carl level so many times before. Our progress was steady until the front end of the jeep began to slam the rear of the bulldozer.

A cemented swimming pool existed when the Wilsons arrived in 1954. The warm water had developed a large amount of algae growth which required considerable cleaning. Carl and a small work crew erected a covered building over the pool during the first winter after resurrecting the old sawmill. The D4 Cat had a power takeoff pulley.

At every bend of the "S" trail Carl carved in the side of the mountain, the trailer jackknifed, each time goring the green metal of the jeep's rear end. Carl guided the Cat carefully, but as we left the grassy slope and snaked into the trees, the trailer rocked back and forth. The trees grew closer together and the rocks bigger.

I knew trouble had come for another visit when Carl shut off the D4. He sat silent for several minutes, scanning the birch and aspen ahead. The boys climbed down from the D4 and headed into the trees.

"If we want to reach the Springs tonight we'll have to leave the jeep," Carl announced.

The underbrush was thick. Saplings, tall grass, and clumps of thorny bushes shielded the boulders and blocked our way. The untarnished beauty of the forest and mountains had become an angry monster of hostility, green and deadly. The wilderness was successfully calling a halt to our trespassing. Carl jumped to the ground and began to unhook the chains from the D4 and the jeep. While I stood there thinking about leaving the jeep behind and how many times we could have turned back had it not been for Carl's determination not to quit, I heard an intense, mourning drone.

"Get the bug juice!" Carl yelled to Mom. He yanked harder on the chain. Dark black and white-striped bodies clouded around us.

"Boys! Get over here and give me a hand!" Rocky and Terry hustled from the trees, carrying long sticks.

Mom rummaged through a paper bag in the back seat of the jeep.

"Yuck! One's in my mouth," Terry said, spitting on the ground.

A government-issued, small bottle passed from hand to hand as limbs, faces and clothing were quickly greased with mosquito repellant. The whining attackers swarmed my head as I waited for the bottle. Mosquitoes flew in my ears and covered my hands. I squeezed my eyes closed and shut my mouth. Carl filled the palm of his hand with repellant and told us to use a lot.

"Here, Gwennie," Mom said, handing the bug dope to me as she waved a leafy branch above my head. It smelled like kerosene, or rubbing alcohol or both. I held my breath and smeared it over any exposed skin, and my clothes, too.

"They're coming up from a swamp," Carl said. "We must be closer to the trail than I thought." When he finished unlinking the two vehicles, I climbed in the jeep and shut the door. I slapped mosquitoes and piled them on the dashboard. They had never been this bad. There were no mosquitos in the mountains, and the ones at Faith Creek were big, and easy to swat. Carl called them snow mosquitoes. The annoying little ones come out later.

When the trailer was secured to the rear of the D4, Carl pushed the jeep to the side of the trail. Mom pulled herself onto the Cat, straddling the fuel tank. In the trailer, we kids snuggled under the tarp that covered our supplies. Topsey and Holly's box hung from one side of the trailer, covered with stiff canvas. Totem waited on his haunches, ears forward.

Carl pulled the cord. The D4 roared. Down the mountain we went, the roar of the D4 bouncing off the mountain. Carl whooped and hollered. I looked back at the jeep. *Just like the swamp buggy,* I thought.

When the incline grew too steep, which was most of the way, everyone but Carl walked. We took turns carrying the kittens. The trailer inched over boulders, rocked back and forth, and landed with a bang but everyone kept moving toward the "old trail," the Chena River's North Fork, and its prized hot springs.

"The old winter trail's not too far after we hit level ground," Carl yelled above the roar.

The trees cracked and slammed the earth with a mighty crash. Rocks rolled to the side. Finally the trees gave way to flatland and swamp. We waded through muddy water that looked like red and green Kool-Aid mixed together. Tall bogs with sticky spears tried to snag us. Finally, soaked and very tired, we trudged onto the ancient trail, long overgrown.

The old trail weaved toward the North Fork, through more spruce and meadows, while the evening sun glowed orange. Around and around went the steel tracks of the D4, clacking a perfect rhythm as the remains of our battered caravan made its way along the valley floor.

Rocky and Terry laid on their bellies, laughing, heads bobbing over the rear of the trailer while Totem hunched between them on the tarp, panting. With my head against the tarp and fingers in both ears so I could hear myself try to sing like Doris Day, I sang every song I knew—even made up one about our journey to the Springs.

A grove of tall spruce loomed ahead and I saw a small boarded-up log cabin surrounded by piles of junk. Carl slowed the D4 to a crawl. Totem leaped to ground. The piles looked important from the way they had been stacked so neatly, probably by trappers. Totem sniffed at the stacks of split logs, gas cans, wooden crates, and mounds of rusted iron parts. He raised his hind leg and marked every one.

"Totem!" shouted Carl. "Cut that out!"

The side of the log cabin displayed saws of different shapes and sizes hanging on rusty nails. A black porkpie hat hung near the weathered door, as if someone had just hung it there on his way inside. Underneath a pole porch we scouted a fishing rod, rubber boots, a couple of rumpled plaid woolen shirts and a frayed, army-issued coat. Was someone there? Probably not with all the windows boarded and a tin can covering the smoke stack.

Stuck around the low crown of the worn out porkpie hat were various fishing flies decorating it like a colored band. Whoever had lived there had to be a good fisherman. An assortment of rusted traps hung on the other side of the door near a small window. It too, was boarded up.

"Red Johnson's place," said Carl. "He traps up here in the winter. Looks as if we missed him; guess he's gone to town."

The D4 clattered on till Carl pulled the right lever of the D4 after rounding a bend where the forest suddenly opened up to a sandbar. We had reached the junction of the North Fork and Monument Creek. One mile to go.

The North Fork was wide. I gripped the sides of the trailer as the D4 entered the river. The water wasn't very deep but the trailer swayed from side to side as it rolled over river rocks.

"Come on, Totem. Atta boy," coaxed Rocky.

"Over here, Totem!" yelled Terry, waving his arms.

Totem followed, belly deep in the easy current. He trotted up the opposite bank, shook his head, behind, then tail, in a funny little dance. River water sprayed off his thick black and gold coat. He loped ahead toward another cabin perched on a small knoll overlooking the two waterways. He sat down and peered back at the D4.

"Another trapper's cabin," Carl hollered. The D4 groaned and crawled out of the North Fork and up an incline toward the small cabin. "Old Sully's place. He's supposed to be buried up there some-where. Walt and Shorty come up in the summer and stay there now."

This cabin faced Monument Creek. The old moss-chinked struc-ture was deserted. A small front window, boarded up like the other cabin, looked out at the old trail where it crossed Monument Creek.

Carl turned the D4 down the bank and across the narrow stream, passing Sully's cabin. I saw a birch sapling growing on the dirt roof, along with other vegetation that sprung from wind-scattered seeds. A gray wooden cross pierced the weeds. Carl was right; somebody was buried up there, but who were Walt and Shorty?

The D4 rumbled around a wooded hill and into a small valley and I remembered the view from the ridge that morning. Totem bolted up the narrow trail and barked when he came upon another, smaller cabin. Though newer than the others, it also was boarded up. Out back, a cache—a miniature log house on high stilts—leaned like it might fall over. A ladder hung horizontally from nails. I would learn later that meant the owner was not at home.

A quarter of a mile to go. The valley widened. Carl pointed back to the big hill. The D4 had carved a perfect "S" on the mountainside where we had come down. Everyone grinned.

The trail angled through a forest of gray trees without bark or leaves, some fallen, where a forest fire once raged, a vivid line marking where the fire had stopped. When the D4 entered green spruce again, I saw a flash through the trees.

"There's the Springs!" I yelled.

The D4 rumbled across Monument Creek and up the other bank till the trees gave way to a large clearing. Nestled together like a small village, surrounded by wooded hills and a clearing, stood a collection of old log buildings, just like I had pictured. I felt like I was stepping into the pages of a storybook. My heart pumped hard as I counted four cabins on either side of the main lodge. Beyond the tiny settlement, near the base of a hill on the other side of the clearing, clouds of steam drifted above the spruce trees and disappeared over the hill.

"There's the steam!" yelled Terry, eyes dancing with delight.

Across a grass-covered landing strip that stretched up toward Far Mountain, we clattered along between the old lodge and what I guessed was the stable. Carl slowed the D4 to a stop. We faced the Lodge as the blade hit the ground. The diesel engine groaned and petered away into silence.

Like a night fog, the eerie desolation from the wilderness crept around us. Carl and Mom climbed down from the D4. The boys and I slipped from the trailer to the ground. The air smelled dead. No one spoke.

High overhead, a loon dove down toward us and laughed. Blue and green swallows chattered about our arrival. They swooped to the supporting structures of the old Lodge and sat watching us in silence. "It's like a ghost town," I whispered.

Carl approached the four evenly-spaced old cabins beside the Lodge. The boys and Totem ran to the swimming pool. I wondered which cabin had been George's, and followed Carl, who checked inside each cabin, then slammed the doors closed.

What is he looking for? There isn't anybody here. The last cabin hadn't survived. The dirt roof lay in the center of what was once the floor, a paddy now crowded with wild seedlings. The remains of the foundation from a fifth cabin, just bits of log carved away by time, were barely visible through the overgrown grass. The old cabins curved like a hunter's bow around the edge of the clearing.

"On the other side of the Lodge are the newer cabins and the old stable," Carl said.

The sun hid behind the hills as we walked past the stable that looked like it was about to fall over. I didn't think it would look so creepy. "Aren't we going to look in there?" I asked.

"Not tonight, Gwennie." Carl checked all the new cabins. They were built of sawed lumber instead of log, painted dark chocolate brown with light blue around the windows. Like the old log cabins on the other side of the Lodge, the newer cabins also circled the clearing, facing a grassy hillside.

"What's that building for?" I asked, pointing to a sagging log cabin on the other side of the swimming pool where Mom and the boys stood.

"The bathhouse. Guess we really are alone. Let's go have a look," he said.

If Carl had known about the condition of the swimming pool, he hadn't let on. Mom had never said anything either. But when I saw the pool I knew there would be no swimming tonight, or tomorrow, or the day after that. Rocky, Terry and I exchanged looks. The boys' gloomy faces spoke of melted expectations. I felt it, too. We said nothing. There was nothing to say.

Scores of colored bugs skimmed the surface of the water. Green and orange algae floated. The algae had grown up the sides of the pool forever and wind-blown junk piled on the bottom.

Carl didn't seem to notice. He led us into the bathhouse and once inside, began explaining about the two separate entrances and bathing areas for the ladies and for the men, each with a dressing room and sunken cement tub.

"Ew, the walls are rotting," I finally spoke aloud.

"From the heat," Carl said.

"Phew!" Terry said, grimacing. "It stinks in here."

"Sulphur," Carl said.

"That's what I smelled outside," said Rocky.

"There's cold water from Spring Creek piped in here too, to cool down the mineral baths."

Rocky and Terry nodded and bolted out of the stinky room.

The old windows needed washing. I saw how the pools drained outside through pipes running through the walls, into a tiny stream that flowed into Spring Creek. Around the pool were scattered wooden mats. Slimy brown algae coated the narrow strips of wood. Against one wall sat a long, moldy bench, waiting. Cement steps led into more dirty water.

I walked to the jeep to let the kittens out. Everything was so drab and forgotten. I wondered what the Lodge looked like on the inside. I followed the boys over to the ponds of hot mineral water. The stench of sulphur grew more intense the closer I got to the pools. I knelt down and dipped my hand into the water. "It's hot!" I screamed, jerking my hand back.

"Dummy," said Rocky. "Of course it's hot. Chena *Hot* Springs."

"Yeah, don't you know anything?" taunted Terry.

I was trying to think of a clever wisecrack when Holly and Topsey scampered up behind me and rubbed against my backside. Then I saw something very strange.

"What are those?"

"What? Where?" Carl asked, stepping closer.

"Those," I said, pointing to the edge of the pool.

Motionless, suspended within the orange and green slime that jiggled in the hot bubbling water, were small, gray worms.

"I'm not sure, Gwennie," Carl said as he knelt down beside me and turned one of the worms over with his finger.

"They have horns," I said. "Ick. How can they live in there?"

The worms were shaped like almonds, very much alive, wriggling the small ridges across their backs. The boys poked the worms with sharp rocks.

"They look prehistoric," said Rocky, cocking his head to one side.

We headed to the old Lodge. Carl pushed on the front door and stepped inside. The door swung wide. Stretching my neck around Carl's waist I looked into a spacious entryway. Mom and the boys trailed in behind us.

Inside, the walls of logs looked the same as they did outside, with ax marks still visible where a logger had peeled off the bark. Old furniture lined the walls, trash covered a dirty wood floor and a large ping-pong table sat in the middle of the room. I felt a chill.

"Did George build the Lodge?" I whispered.

"Part of it, Gwennie," Carl said softly.

The room smelled of stale ashes and musty neglect. Rocky and Terry ran over to the ping-pong table.

"Looks like somebody decorated for a party," Mom said, standing in the middle of the room, staring up at the ceiling. Vines of toilet paper draped between the log-beam ceiling poles.

"Squirrels," Carl said. His eyes scanned the room. He walked promptly to a doorway at the far end of the room and disappeared down a hallway.

For as long as I can remember we were always told not to go into anyone's house when there was no one at home. This was different, I knew, because it wasn't really somebody's house. Still, someone who lived here had stepped out of this room and never returned, leaving behind all they owned in the whole world. I felt sad thinking of the owners abandoning this project like we left the swamp buggy and then the jeep.

The room looked familiar, from the way Carl explained how pioneers built their first homes. The log walls were chinked with moss, old rags and hard-dried mud and sawdust to keep the winter out. Vinyl couches sat alone beneath large windows—a red one, a dark green one, and one Mom called "ugly lime." Dusty floor lamps topped with cream-colored shades still protected by cellophane wrappings stood guard for each couch.

Some of the chinking from between the logs had fallen onto the uneven wooden floor, scarred from years of foot traffic. Sunlight seeped through wide cracks between the logs. The nearly fifty-year-old boards creaked beneath my sneakers as I stepped over a torn *Ladies Home Companion* magazine, rags, newspapers, empty brown Budweiser bottles and more toilet paper. I hesitated near the ping-pong table in the middle of the room. Toilet paper draped the table and trailed onto an old-fashioned wood chair.

"Wow," Terry said. He had picked up a paddle. Rocky tossed a ping-pong ball his way and they batted it back and forth across a ragged net.

"Not now, boys," Carl said from a second doorway across the room. Then, more to himself than to us he added, "That table's got to go."

An enormous oil barrel that sat at the end of the room, supported by heavy iron legs, had been turned on its side to serve as a wood stove. A rusty stovepipe pierced the rough beams and the ceiling. Underneath the barrel stove, sheets of tin had been nailed to the floor. A small window draped with faded curtains let in enough light for me to see a tall, dusty counter and cash register.

"The bar," Carl said, reaching for some papers laying on the counter. Dirty glasses, empty beer cans, and old ledgers littered the countertop. Shelves behind the bar stored cloudy glasses turned upside-down in front of two small wood-framed mirrors nailed to the dirty log wall. Underneath was a small refrigerator.

Holding the papers in one hand, Carl poked his head into the dining room. I could see more toilet paper across a worn linoleum dining room floor. The walls were covered with light blue cheesecloth, and in some places the blue paint had peeled away to expose a dull green earlier paint job. The ceiling sagged over an old dining table with straight-backed chairs.

"Big enough for a couple of tables, don't you think, Belle?" He glanced at the ping-pong table. "We can serve a lot of people in here."

I stepped into the dining room to find an iron bed covered with brown sheets and a wool blanket shoved against a wall near a window. Toilet paper wrapped the bed and the nearby Yukon stove. I retreated to the big room and stood near a poker table near the bar, spying glasses full of dead bugs on the dirty green felt top, thin from years of leaning elbows and long hours of placing bets. Chairs held heaps of magazines and newspapers littered the table. Even older yellow newspapers peeked at me through holes in the felt.

How could we live here? This was not at all what I had expected. On the wall, two framed newspaper articles hung by nails. One article listed the contents of the hot mineral water, and the other relayed the history of George Wilson's homestead.

"What does p-a-t-e-n-t mean?" I asked as Mom walked up behind me.

"Means he owned the land. But there was a battle that went on for many years. They tried to take the homestead away from him."

"Why?"

"Because he was a Canadian," Carl said, entering the room, "among other things." He handed the papers he'd been carrying around to Mom. "Save these," he said. He took the ledgers from the bar and gave those to her also.

"Why would they take away his homestead just because he was from Canada? Who tried to take it away? What 'other things'?" I asked.

"Rocky, get the lantern," Carl said, leaving my question hanging. He walked around the barrel stove and pulled a large silver ring like a door-knocker, nailed to the floor. Rocky ran to the trailer for the lantern. The floor opened up to a dirt cellar. Carrying a lighted Coleman lantern, Carl stepped down a rickety wooden stairway into a hole beneath the floor and I followed close behind.

"It's cold down here," I said, hugging myself, keeping very close to Carl. I saw ghost-like images dance on the dirt walls behind the log floor supports.

"What's down there?" Terry yelled from above.

Rocky said, "Ghosts. Maybe some bears. Sic 'em, Totem!"

"There are not!" I yelled back.

"There's been somebody here, all right," Carl shouted, investigating some cardboard boxes on a dirt ledge near the back wall. "There's still a little food here," he said, handing me boxes of dried macaroni. He collected the cans of soup and vegetables, and we climbed back up the stairs.

I found four bedrooms and two small bathrooms off the hallway of the main room. All of them had smooth white-painted walls like our house in town. The squirrels had torn the mattresses to shreds. Along with foam stuffing there were pillow feathers and more toilet paper everywhere. Behind a Yukon stove at the end of the hall I could see George's stable through a small, dirty window.

The kitchen, adjacent to the dining room, had open shelves stacked with old restaurant plates, bowls, cups, saucers, pie plates, serving bowls and platters. I had never seen so many dishes. In one corner of the room was a black cast iron army cook range, cluttered with dirty pots and pans. This room also had a ceiling that sagged and a long messy work counter lining two walls. A third wall held a double metal sink under the window near the back door. More pots and pans crusted with leftover moldy food waited in one of the sinks for help.

"What an awful mess," Mom said leaning up against the doorway of the laundry room, hands stuffed deep inside her jean pockets. She looked sleepy.

"It won't take long to get this place in shape," Carl said.

How could that be true? The mice and squirrels had turned the pantry upside down, floors white with flour, rice and sugar. The laundry room off the kitchen was in disarray where linens, cleaning supplies, a wringer washing machine and what was left of the toilet paper were stored. I expected Carl to tell a joke about the dirty pans or why the squirrels used up all the toilet paper. Even if he had said we were welcome to go swim with the bugs, I would have laughed and believed that making the Lodge our cozy home for the summer was possible. His reassurance would have made all the difference in the world.

"Boys, start unloading the gear in front of the second cabin below the stable," Carl ordered.

Mom turned and headed for the front door of the Lodge. I walked with the boys, thinking of all the people Carl had said were coming to eat dinner and how the ceiling in the dining room was barely suspended over their dinner plates. I wondered which of the four bedrooms with ripped up mattresses was going to be my very own.

Mom swept out the second cabin below George's stable. The boys and I brought in the camping gear. While Mom stripped the cots of dirty sheets and blankets, the boys built a fire in the Yukon stove, then fetched water from Spring Creek. After a bowl of hot soup, I called the kittens.

"They stay outside," Carl said, putting their box on the back end of the trailer. "They can sleep in there if they want to."

Resting on a cot atop a sleeping bag in the midnight light, I prepared a mental list of all the things to investigate in the morning. It was like counting a huge flock of sheep, I suppose, because the next thing I knew it was morning.

CHAPTER 14

Clean-Up

———

Birds, millions of birds, yakked outside the cabin while blinding sun rays streamed through a dirty window. I rubbed my eyes, trying to decide whether to go to the stable first or the Lodge when I caught sight of two black eyes the size of pinpoints. Thoughts of exploration fizzled. Balancing on the edge of a small spotlight of sunshine on the wall beside me crouched a big, ugly spider.

Fear gripped me. Could I escape the creepy-crawly? Maybe I could grab something and smack it before it bit me. From the corner of my eye I saw Mom and Carl, still asleep. Rocky and Terry also slept, sprawled on top of their sleeping bags on the floor like garden scarecrows toppled by the wind.

Sunshine flickered back and forth across the black spider's furry legs. I quietly slid out of my sleeping bag and pulled on my jeans. Shivers darted down my back. *Ugh, how eerie!* The spider scurried up the wall and into a corner. Shirt untucked, I stepped over Rocky and Terry, snatched my glasses from the wooden washstand, jammed a tube of toothpaste and my toothbrush in my jeans pocket and headed out the door.

The morning smelled of flowers. Across the meadow near Spring Creek, robins hopped. Near the center of the grassy meadow were more robins, tugging on their breakfast in the loose soil while noisy ocean-colored swallows sat wing to wing on the electrical wires leading from the stable. Holly and Topsey chased butterflies in the grass near the stoop. Beautiful butterflies!

A door hinge moaned. A loon somewhere up the airfield yodeled, and I glanced back at Carl, still sleeping like the others. If I could get outside before anyone woke up, I'd be the first one up—a good joke on Carl, who was usually up first. I gently closed the door and latched it this time.

A single butterfly, resting in a patch of dirt a few feet of the cabin doorstep, proudly fluttered its yellow and black wings. Before I could get close to it, Holly scampered ahead of me. Off flew the butterfly, carrying both its beauty and its fears far above the ground, into the safety of the blue expanse.

I darted through the high grass, wishing I could see Carl's face when he opened his eyes and found my mattress empty. Clover higher than my knees covered the path behind the third cabin. The kittens were hot on my tail, and the bees hummed, perched on pink clover blossoms. I slammed the outhouse door behind me. "Yea! I'm the first one up."

The latrine hole was deep. Flies buzzed over lumpy stuff in the bottom but the place didn't smell too bad. I did my duty and quickly left. Topsey and Holly, their tails straight up, trotted behind me all the way to Spring Creek. As we neared the water's edge, something—a twig, maybe—snapped beside me. I studied the hillside cautiously, but whatever had been there was gone. I brushed my teeth facing the hillside, just in case.

As I stood to return to the cabin, a movement in the water caught my eye. A big, gray fish darted through the water. It hovered a moment above the creek stones, then slowly moved upstream a short ways and hovered again. A large unblinking eye on the side of its head peered through the ripples at me.

I had never been this close to a wild fish. It blended into the bottom of the stream like a rock. It fluttered its tail, unafraid, its fins waving in the water like fans. It was as beautiful and free as the butterfly.

Lucy the moose became a familiar sight at the Springs. After a year or two she felt safe enough to bring her calf along to enjoy our clover patch.

Just then a cabin door slammed. Carl in the lead with a bucket, followed by the boys, marched across the meadow. The fish zigzagged up the creek and out of sight.

Dipping the bucket into Spring Creek, Carl said, "He'll be back. Probably was a grayling." Carl went back to the cabin.

"Bet you didn't even see one," Rocky hollered at me from upstream.

"I did, too. If you hadn't scared it off you'd have seen it." I figured the fish would never come back, so I walked back to the cabin leaving Rocky and Terry to race along the bank of the creek looking for the fish.

Mom already had a fire going in the stove. She had mixed up flour and water for pancakes and asked me to watch the fire while she went to the creek to brush her teeth. When we returned, we made sugar syrup with Mapleine, maple flavoring we brought with us.

I ate breakfast in silence. Carl wouldn't stop talking long enough for me to tell him I had been the first one up that morning. He went on and on about how we would paint the dining room when we got through cleaning it, and why a lot of people would fly in to the Springs for the Fourth of July because there weren't many places to go to around Fairbanks on the holidays. He said the boys had to help chop wood for the kitchen stove every day so Mom could cook and I had to help her.

"I was the first one up this morning," I blurted out. I could no longer hold it in.

Carl wiped a thick layer of butter across his second stack of pancakes in the middle of his plate. "Oh, I was awake."

I felt my eyebrows rise to the top of my forehead. "No, you weren't," I said. Carl half-grinned at me.

The boys smirked but for once didn't make any smart remarks. It seemed a very long time to me before anyone said anything. Any other time I would have gotten a stern lecture from Carl about saying "no" to him. I expected it at any moment, but Carl just asked Mom for more syrup.

Carl, Gwen and Belle relax at the Lodge with young visitors Jimmy and Ricky Gray on a summer afternoon.

"Awake even before the birds," Carl said in a sing-song voice, pouring syrup over his pancakes. Hunks of butter slid off the stack and whirled around the plate. "Just thought I'd take it easy and lounge in bed awhile this morning."

"When I woke up, I heard the birds singing," Rocky said.

"You weren't awake, either," I said. "Everybody was asleep. Nobody was awake."

Carl grinned at me again, rose from the table and started for the door. "Better get a grocery list ready, Belle. We're only thirty minutes by plane from Fairbanks. People will take advantage of that and come here. Takes people all day to drive to Circle Hot Springs. Pack a lunch. We're going back up the Big Hill for the jeep today." He left the cabin.

When the dishes were done I made a beeline for George's stable. I assumed I would have the whole day to look around but there was little time to explore. Carl made a new hitch for the jeep out of pipes he found in the stable. By midmorning we were on our way back up the last hill with the D4.

I was straddled in front of Mom on the fuel tank, worried about the kittens now left alone in a strange place. I was still sulking a bit that my plan to explore the stable got postponed. Rocky and Terry started squirming in the black seat next to Carl. All the way up the mountain they took turns yelling at Totem not to go too far ahead, and goading each other.

By early afternoon when we reached the jeep I was really anxious. Lunch settled me down well enough, but like before, we struggled to get down the Big Hill to the swamp and the old trail before the sun set.

The D4 dragged the jeep over large round bogs. Carl kept shoveling black muck from around the jeep tires and pulling debris from the bulldozer tracks. When we arrived at the Springs, Chuck Gray's plane was parked at the lower end of the runway near the Lodge. It was late at night.

"Saw you coming off the big hill when I flew in," Chuck said. "Thought you were just arriving. If you hadn't built that fire the other night on the trail, I might still be looking for you."

At the cabin, Mom built a fire and heated up soup. Carl told Chuck about the ten-day trek across the mountains. His version of the wild ride backwards into Frozenfoot Creek caused my stomach to rumble as fears from that day returned. When Carl told him a black bear chased him and Rocky up the mountain, Chuck laughed. Everybody did; it was funny now.

"Any chance you can go back up with me to get the swamp buggy?" Carl asked Chuck.

"I'd like to, but I can't take time off from work. I could bring a friend up to help, though. I'll ask Ronnie."

Carl nodded. "Belle and the kids can start cleaning the Lodge while we're gone."

Mom scribbled out a grocery list on the back of a soup can label. "Anything that's too badly stained, can't be fixed or washed, or is just plain junk is going in the trash," Mom said, referring to random items littering the whole Lodge.

Rocky and Terry headed for the cabin door. "Don't wander off, boys!" Carl hollered.

"We're going to find Totem," Rocky said.

"And look behind the old cabins," Terry said, his eyes wide. "There's a lot of stuff back there."

Carl nodded his head in approval and the boys scurried out the door. "I figure this cabin can be a cook cabin until we can move into the Lodge," he told Chuck. "Gwen and the boys can sleep here. Belle and I are going to take the first cabin. There used to be more cabins. I found some of the old foundations."

He reached under one of beds for the ledgers he had found in the big room of the Lodge. Chuck was familiar with the Springs before Carl bought it.

"There's a fellow by the name of Jim Stanley," Chuck said, looking over Carl's shoulder as he turned the yellowed pages of the ledger, reading signatures from long ago. Chuck continued, "Jim spends the winters up here. He knew Colfax Gregg and George Wilson. In fact, Jim still uses Gregg's old cabin down the river sometimes." Chuck went on to explain that his family, the Grays, lived next door to Gregg in Graehl when they first came to Fairbanks in 1943. Gregg had a large single-room log cabin with a sousaphone horn hanging on the back wall. He said Gregg once played in a circus band. Later, he spent years cutting timber on the North Fork for the Independent Mill in town, so he made numerous trips up and down the Chena. He is buried down near Angel Rocks.

I was stretched out on one of the beds listening to all of this. It was hard to imagine what it would be like to meet someone who knew someone who actually knew George Wilson himself. Weird!

"Shame the place hasn't been kept up," Carl said. "The swimming pool and bathhouse are going to be the toughest to clean. The bathhouse needs a lot of repairs."

Mom said, "I hope the washing machine works."

"When I get back with the swamp buggy I'll crank up the light plant (our generator) and we'll find out," Carl assured her. Carl had an old single cylinder Witte engine with a heavy flywheel hooked to a generator using belts. A governor on the engine maintained an even speed by shutting the diesel fuel on and off. We hadn't used it in awhile.

On Thursday and Friday, Mom and I swept winter dust from the first and third cabins below George's stable. Carl spent the whole time tweaking the D4 for the trip back up the Big Hill. The boys and I carried utensils, cookware, more soup and packages of noodles from the Lodge to the second cabin. Carl and Mom moved into the first cabin and Chuck's friend, Ronnie, who was coming Friday night, would get to use cabin three.

I was not pleased to be sharing the second cabin with Rocky and Terry again.

"Who's going to sleep on the floor?" Rocky asked.

"I certainly don't want to sleep on the floor," I said.

"So how would you know what it's like, sleeping on the floor?" Rocky asked.

"Yeah. Since you haven't slept on the floor, it's your turn," Terry said.

I said, "We should draw straws like Mom always has us do."

"We don't have any straws," Terry said. "How about little sticks?"

"I'll go get some." Rocky bound out the door.

In the first place, I suppose they were still angry because Mom hadn't ordered cookies. In the second place, Rocky and Terry had already made up their minds about whose turn it was to sleep on the floor. I drew the shortest stick, no big surprise.

When Chuck flew Ronnie in, he also brought boxes full of groceries. The boys didn't say anything when we unpacked the parcels, but I could tell they were disappointed. Mom had ordered Kool-Aid, coffee, canned milk, tuna fish, peanut butter, eggs, butter, and bread. Chuck also toted two weeks' worth of mail. No jelly, hot chocolate, or marshmallows, and no meat of any kind because there was no way to keep it until Carl got the light plant going. We would have ham and bacon when Carl returned with the swamp buggy.

Early Saturday morning the boys and I helped carry gear to the D4 as Carl and Ronnie prepared for the trip back up the big hill to get the buggy. Ronnie lifted the metal food can packed with soup and tools over his head and handed it up to Carl like it was a cardboard box. He was younger than Chuck, short and stocky, and laughed at everything Carl said even when it wasn't funny. He carried the biggest chains over his arms like they were jump-ropes. Carl always dragged them behind him on the ground.

After the men were gone, Mom led the way to the Lodge. We opened the doors and windows wide so that fresh air from the valley could circulate throughout the building, flushing out all the sad, musty smells. For the next five days the tasks were many and the workdays long.

Mom assigned the boys and me specific jobs. The boys dismantled the iron bed in the dining room and dragged the parts outside. They set aside broken chairs for Carl to repair. Terry wandered from room to room, rolling up toilet paper while Rocky carried boxes of trash to a spot behind the kitchen.

My first job was the pantry off the kitchen. I made cleaning into a game. I worked quickly, stacking canning jars in boxes and scrubbing the pantry shelves with soap and hot water that Rocky and Terry toted in from the bathhouse. Carl would be surprised if everything was done when he got back. I wanted to freshen up the pantry shelves with some paint I'd seen in the stable. Mom said maybe later.

Mom and I discussed the laundry room mice that had made nests in the sheets and blankets. Must've been cozy, compared to their other options. We sorted all the linens by color and stacked them in the dining room in big piles to be washed. I rearranged the shelves with unopened packages of toilet paper and cleaning supplies. Mom spent most of her time in the kitchen.

"What are *those*?" I pinched my nose shut with two fingers. "It smells awful." Soft-bodied, white, legless creatures wiggled through gray-green looking stuff in the bottom of some of the pots Mom had placed in the kitchen sink.

"Maggots," Mom said. "Baby flies. I've been scraping and scraping at this moldy food with this wooden spoon too long. Whoever made this mess should have had the decency to clean it up."

She finally grabbed the handle of the pot and marched outside holding it at arm's length. I did the same with a smaller pot, exaggerating my movements so I looked like her. We both burst out laughing. The thought of those ugly things crawling up my arm had made me feel like throwing up, but somehow we found a way to laugh about it.

Every morning before we had breakfast, and every evening after supper, a cow—which means female—moose paid a visit to the hot water ponds on the other side of the bathhouse near Spring Creek. The four of us staring didn't seem to bother the moose. Mom said the cow was coming in for the clover. Aside from watching the moose chew clover, the boys and I had little time to play.

One afternoon the boys went for more hot water and wandered off to Spring Creek to play cowboys and Indians. Grim-faced, Mom sat them down along with me because she had found me the day before, preoccupied with the wooden blueberry pickers and ancient black clothes irons in the laundry room. We were given a lengthy talking-to about distractions and sticking to our jobs for the day.

We heard the Cat clatter up the valley long before it rolled in with the swamp buggy. The boys ran out immediately. They jumped up and down on the edge of the airfield, smirking like clowns, eager to greet Carl and Ronnie.

On the way to the cabin I told Carl about the mice having their pinkies in the laundry room. Rocky and Terry wrinkled up their noses and made disgusting sounds. Talk of babies always grossed them out.

"Did you get the food?" Rocky asked.

"You should have seen it, Carl," I went on, glaring at the boys. "All the blankets were stained with yellow. They peed on the sheets and pillowcases, left little black things all over everything. Mom said she didn't know if it would come out in the wash or not, but we piled everything in the dining room."

"You did a fine job, Gwennie," he said, patting me on the back. "You boys did, too," he said, though they didn't help us with the laundry at all.

At the cabin Mom poured a can of vegetable soup into a small pot and placed it on the stove next to a pot with macaroni cooking. It reminded me of the maggots in the kitchen.

"What did you think of the trip and Carl's trail?" Mom asked Ronnie.

Ronnie laughed. "Only crazy people do things like that."

Rocky asked, "Did you get the food?"

Mom grabbed the pot of macaroni from the stove and scooted out the door just beyond the cabin to pour off the boiling water.

"What about the food, Carl?" Rocky asked again.

Mom returned and poured hot soup over the macaroni.

"Yeah! Where's all the food we left up there?" Terry said.

Carl took a deep breath. "When we got to the buggy we found the canvas we left over the supplies on the ground a few yards away ripped to shreds. Most everything in the swamp buggy was destroyed or packed off. I'm afraid the bacon and hams," Carl paused, "are no more. That bear must have had a feast before he left."

Ronnie laughed again. "He even chewed his way into the canned stuff," he said, scratching his head.

"There wasn't much left to salvage," Carl said.

"No food at all?" Terry asked.

144

"No food," said Carl.

Mom cut camp bread into squares and dished up supper. Chuck was scheduled to pick up Ronnie on Sunday evening. On Friday and Saturday we cleaned George's stable. Behind the kitchen we stacked furniture that Carl said was beyond repair. At Mom's suggestion, we switched all the beds around and heaped all the smelly mattresses on the junk pile. She prepared another grocery list.

We greeted Sunday morning with bowls of Cream-O-Wheat. The cold cereal was gone and we were tired of pancakes and syrup made with white sugar and flavored with Mapleine. Rocky and Terry turned up their noses at the pitcher of diluted evaporated milk.

"It's your choice. Eat it or go hungry," Mom said.

Carl said, "When we're done cleaning and that pile behind the kitchen is taller than I am, you boys can take the little Oliver in the stable and haul away the junk with the trailer."

"We get to drive the 'little Cat!'" Terry said to Rocky. The boys gobbled down their hot cereal and evaporated milk and left the cabin.

"They will build a mountain," Mom said to Carl. Ronnie chuckled.

"Yeah, I know. Come on, Ron. Let go see if we can crank up the light plant."

Later that evening as the sun slid behind the hill and the swallows lined up side by side on the electric wires, Chuck flew in. "I'll try and get those groceries up by the middle of the week, Belle," he said and slipped her grocery list into his shirt pocket.

We gathered at the end of the runway to bid our goodbyes to Ronnie and Chuck. Carl said, "Having trouble getting that light plant to run. When you return I might have to send in an order for parts. Can't seem to find the problem yet."

We watched Chuck taxi up the runway and turn the plane around to take off. Knowing it would be several days before his return terrified me. The small amount of food we had left just didn't seem to me to be enough to last until then. As the days passed in anticipation of Chuck's return I found the waiting irritating. I wasn't sure what Mom had written on the grocery list, and I had no trouble thinking of many good things we could be eating. Now I was in suspense as to what would come in the next load.

By the middle of the week Carl had not been successful in getting the light plant started. He worked up a sweat but his many tugs on the starter rope had produced nothing more than pitiful chug... chug...chug-a-chugs. The boys now had to carry hot water to the cabin, since we couldn't yet heat it.

"My clothes smell funny," Terry said.

"You smell funny," Rocky said.

Carl said, "Everyone needs a hot bath, so no more complaining from either of you. Until the light plant is running and the bath-house and swimming pool are cleaned you'll just have to remember why we all smell."

Mom said, "There's so much—sheets, blankets, bedspreads, towels. It will take days to wash and dry it all. We won't have the cabins ready by the Fourth."

"Once we get the generator running it will go quickly, Belle," Carl assured her.

Rocky and Terry snickered when Mom hung her undies up to dry from nails on the outside wall of the cabin. The generator would operate the wringer washer, the pump in the cellar for cold water to the bathrooms in the Lodge, and another pump on the platform of the swimming pool for draining the pools so we could clean them and take a bath.

By Friday afternoon Mom and I had cleaned our way into the four bedrooms off the big room in the Lodge. I was sweeping mattress stuffing and pillow feathers into little heaps when Mom started to joke about the dirty toilet bowls in the bathrooms off the hallway. "Having to squat for ten days in the woods while we were on the trail was far worse than using these outhouses," she reminded me.

Sitting over a big hole was creepy, but I agreed. Even though I could fall in, the earth-closets beat squatting in the woods with mosquitos biting your bottom. Unfortunately, both outhouses had begun to stink since the days had turned warmer, particularly the two-seater behind the old cabins.

We had peas on macaroni for supper. Mom mentioned she was ready to mop the floors in the Lodge and start washing all the dishes as soon as we were done eating.

"Green pea spaghetti sauce?" joked Carl.

Mom said, "It's a new recipe," with her hand on her hip like Betty Crocker and a look that said this is the way it is. Rocky and Terry made monster faces. Chuck didn't come that evening, but no one mentioned it.

I carried the leftovers to the kerosene crate Carl had set in the frigid flow of Spring Creek and looked for the big gray fish. Again, tonight, there was no sign of him. I hadn't seen him since the morning we arrived. I shoved the can of butter aside to make room for the bowl of noodles, taking extra care not to block the holes on either end of the wooden box and block the creek water. I walked the grassy bank to find another flat rock to secure the lid. I studied the creek one more time in hopes of seeing graylings, when all of a sudden I heard a roar bellow from the stable.

Chug...chug...chug...putt, putt, putt, putt...faster and faster. The sound knocked into every corner of the valley and echoed off the side hill. I rushed into the stable just as Carl flipped on the main switch. The rush of mechanical energy converted into electrical energy traveled through the wires from the stable into the Lodge, into all the cabins' light bulbs and pumps. Carl turned toward me, smiling as the light bulb over his head glowed brightly, like this was his good idea. "Now Mom can wash the laundry!" he hollered above the roar.

"I'm going to clean the restrooms in the morning," I shouted and raced to the cabin.

"How about a fishing trip?" Carl asked later as the boys and I crawled into our sleeping bags. "This has been a big project. We've worked hard. I'll be glad when we get the bathtubs and swimming pool cleaned. Even though there's lots of hard work left to do, I was thinking about a trip down to the North Fork."

147

"Mom and I'll pack something to eat," I said. Rocky and Terry bobbed their heads up and down and exchanged a glance that said they didn't think it would be much of a picnic.

We didn't have much food yet, but we did have electricity. Carl mounted the light plant on a solid log platform but still it seemed to want to tear itself loose every time we ran it. Carl later secured it to a heavy cement platform about a foot thick, and that did the trick. For the next year, that old Witte engine powered our family's thorough overhaul of the resort. Inch by inch, we cleaned up the old structures and built new ones. Carl hired a small crew of experienced woodsmen who stayed all winter, helping us prepare Chena Hot Springs for its re-opening day, a little over a month away.

CHAPTER 15

Where No One Walked

––––––––

The boys had the giggles. Carl told them three times to quiet down and eat their breakfast but whatever prompted their silliness was definitely more powerful than Carl's commands. I had suspected something was up when Terry kept squinting at me like he knew something. And Rocky rolled his eyes so many times it started to annoy me.

I cleaned the restrooms in the Lodge right after breakfast. Next I went to the kitchen to get a head start on washing the dishes before Mom came up from the cabin, as a surprise. Mom said she wanted all the dishes washed and back on the open shelves before lunchtime. I thought no further of the boys' behavior that morning until they strutted through the back door of the kitchen, snickering.

"Guess what," whispered Rocky.

"What," I said, reaching for another stack of bowls from the shelves near the laundry room. Rocky smiled like he had gotten a whiff of something really bad. I set the bowls on the table and reached for another stack.

"Guess," Rocky said.

"She'll never guess," Terry said with a sneer.

"Guess," he said again.

"I don't know!...You found something dead?"

"No!"

"You act like you did. Carl was really mad at you guys this morning. What was so funny?"

"We snuck out of the cabin this morning," Rocky said, "when everyone was still asleep and...."

"And pushed the washing machine over to the swimming pool," Terry interrupted.

"You did not," I said, laughing.

"I wanted to tell it," Rocky yelled at Terry.

"Did, too," Rocky insisted. "Mom can wash clothes now."

I looked in the laundry room. Sure enough, the machine was gone. I knew full well that if Carl hadn't agreed to this idea of theirs beforehand Rocky and Terry were in big trouble. "Did Carl say you could do it?"

Rocky said, "No. Besides, then it wouldn't be a surprise. Anyway, he won't care."

The boys hastened to the front door of the Lodge. "We're going to go tell Carl," Terry shouted over his shoulder.

I set another stack of bowls on the table and followed them outside. Carl was tightening wires around a wooden pole for another clothes-line. Rocky told his story in detail. I worried about how Carl might react when Rocky finished informing him of their little surprise.

"You did, huh? Must have been quite a job for the two of you," Carl said without looking up.

Cocky grins appeared on both the boys' faces, intended for me. Nevertheless, I was taken aback by Carl's easy-going reaction, given that we had always been told to get Carl's permission before taking on a major mission like this one. So now Carl didn't care that the boys attempted this project on their own. *Okay*, I thought. *That's new.*

"Well, go get your Mom!" Carl said, putting his tools on the ground.

Like two of the seven dwarfs from Snow White, off they marched to a lively tune no one else heard. The boys were back in no time, leading all of us across the rocky path of weeds between the Lodge and bathhouse, on to the swimming pool.

"Should put a walkway here," Carl assessed, escorting Mom.

I tagged along behind, encouraged about moving into the Lodge tomorrow if we could wash and dry enough sheets today. I was looking forward to having my own room again.

"When did you boys do this?" Mom squealed when she saw the white enamel machine sitting on the platform by the hot water pipe. The boys told their story all over again while Carl went for an extension cord.

"Flip the switch, Belle," Carl said when he had plugged the extension cord into the light fixture above the door of the men's bath and dragged it across the cement platform to plug into the washer. The Springs already had an ancient generator.

Mom glanced at the foul bedding stacked across the platform of the pool. Her fingers pushed the switch to the on position.

Nothing happened. Carl examined the outlet in the light fixture. He inspected the motor of the washer and the extension cord connections.

"Try it again, Belle," he said. The motor did not start.

"What's wrong with it?" Rocky wailed, disappointed.

"Not sure," Carl said, shaking his head.

Rocky and Terry's big surprise had flopped.

"Going to have to work on it awhile."

Back in the kitchen, steam spiraled upward from large soup kettles. Mom poked at the fire in the army range with a poker until she had leveled a bed of bright red coals.

"First the light plant, now the washer," she said, throwing three sticks of wood into the firebox of the stove. "What could possibly happen next? We'll never make it by the Fourth of July at this rate. Never."

The dry spruce kindling we had gathered from a nearby hillside ignited quickly. Mom poured hot water from one of the kettles into the dishpan, refilled the kettle with cold water and returned it to the stove to heat. She had tied a large ratty dishtowel around her waist.

"There's just too much left to do and it all depends on that darn washing machine!"

Silently, I admired the many towers of cups, glasses, bowls, pots, plates, pans and silverware I'd stacked on the table like buildings in a little city. It hadn't taken me long to stack them up.

"There's enough dinnerware here to serve an army at a sit-down supper," Mom said as she emptied another kettle of hot water into a second dishpan she had prepared with a disinfecting solution. Mom washed and I dried, as I talked about George living at the Hot Springs a long time ago, having to go to town for supplies, how much food he must have had to buy at one time. I wanted to know if George had cows and how old the dishes were and if the dishes were George's and if he had a hard time getting all those dishes up the river. I asked Mom how many trips he made.

"I don't know, Gwennie!" she snapped and grabbed another stack of blue-trimmed saucers from the city of dishes and plunged them into the soapy water. "It's too hot in here," she said. Seeing Mom's irritability and her in-no-mood-for-conversation attitude, I decided to ask about George's life at the Springs later.

By early evening Carl still had not succeeded in getting the washing machine to work. I lifted the last dish from the pan of disinfectant solution, dried it and set it on an open shelf with the others. Mom mopped the floor in silence.

I had enjoyed cleaning the Lodge in preparation for the Fourth. I wanted Mom to be excited, too. The washing machine wasn't working but the pump at the bathhouse was. At least we could clean out the swimming pool and the baths when Carl got done pumping out all the dirty water. I stepped back to admire the many dishes I had dried in one day.

A few moments later a plane zoomed over the top of the Lodge. I ran to the kitchen window in time to see the plane turn sharply to the left and bank against the hill at the upper end of the valley. Evening sun rays spotlighted the markings of a Cessna 170.

"It's Chuck!" I yelled as the plane disappeared behind the treetops, on approach to the runway. I bolted out the back door and ran to the edge of the runway to wait for Chuck to taxi down the field.

The boys and Carl hastened from the swimming pool. Chuck swung the tail of the plane a half-circle before rolling to a halt. He unloaded boxes of groceries onto the edge of the runway. "I brought fresh lettuce, tomatoes and meat for the Fourth," he said as he announced he was going to make yet another trip this evening. Chuck had made a deal with Carl to make at least one supply trip each week during the summer to help us get started.

Carl scribbled out a list of parts for the washer and handed it to him. "I'll have an advertisement for the *News-Miner* about the re-opening of the Springs when you return," Carl said.

Mom grabbed a sack of oranges and apples. "Put the pickles and olives in the cooler off the kitchen, Gwennie." She headed for the kitchen.

It was like a Christmas morning, opening all the parcels of food after Chuck flew back to town. I carried four cartons of eggs at a time into the damp darkness of the cellar below the Lodge. The small flashlight I carried strained for power in the dimness. I shivered in dread, even though I knew there weren't any Slubbertails down there. I hadn't seen any fuzz balls anywhere. I only saw the shadows of the log pilings holding up the floor and my shadow drifting along the dirt walls through the cobwebs. The water pump was quiet. I returned to the cellar three more times, then took the butter to the cold box at Spring Creek.

The pride in what we had accomplished since our arrival was as great as the feast Mom served from the old table in the log kitchen the next evening; bowls of buttered canned corn and canned meat and gravy, mashed potatoes, lots of Kool-aid and a lettuce and tomato salad. Carl told a joke about a chicken crossing the road to get to the other side and the boys started laughing. But Mom's concern about the dirty laundry resurfaced.

"What on earth are we going to do?" she asked Carl. "We won't be able to move to the Lodge if I can't make the beds."

She forewarned of several horrifying situations that would result from the dismantled washing machine being out of service. And of course there would be no swim towels or swimsuits to rent on the

Fourth of July. Where in the world could she possibly hide the heaps of dirty laundry so the guests wouldn't see them?

Rocky swirled gravy over the mashed potatoes heaped in the middle of his plate. "There's a washing machine in the trees," he practically whispered.

"Yeah!" clamored Terry. "We found it that day we looked though all the junk behind the old cabins."

"It's behind the cabin that's all caved in," Rocky said, "back in the trees. There's a bunch of other stuff back there, too." He stacked his fork with potatoes and aimed at his mouth.

"It's wood," Terry said. "Looks rotten."

"It isn't rotten. It just looks rotten," Rocky mumbled.

"We'll go have a look tomorrow," said Carl. He didn't look excited. Everyone could tell.

In the morning before the swallows could gather on the power lines, Rocky and Terry made like soldiers, leading the way to a patch of woods behind the old cabins. Among the dense weeds and tall grass, in the shadow of the old trees, a wooden washing machine lay on its side near three old, rusted horse-drawn plows.

I knew the plows had belonged to George. George used them before someone threw them back there and forgot about them. The sight stirred a great sadness in me as I wondered if someday the things I treasured most would end up in a place where no one walked, like George's things.

"Whoever dumped this stuff out here didn't think they needed it anymore, I guess," Carl said. "Must have been a long time ago."

He pulled the brush back and inspected the washer that was once white, like my new tennis shoes. The wooden tubs were splintered and ash gray from years exposed to the weather. Four sturdy legs made of straight pieces of thick, sawed lumber supported double wood basins and a loosely fitted wooden wringer with a hand crank.

Carl grabbed one side of the washer. "Let's turn it right side up, boys!" Rocky and Terry grabbed the other side. With a heavy thrust the three of them lifted the washer out of the weeds and flipped it over.

154

Moss blotched the side that had hugged the dirty ground for all those years. Spiders even laced the inside with webs that displayed an impressive collection of dead bugs.

"Well," Carl said, "it's old, that's for sure. No telling how long it's been here. This moss says a long time, but you never know. It just might work. Let's give her a try."

"Good thing we told you, huh?" asked Terry.

"Good thing I told him," Rocky corrected.

Mom watched from the apron of the pool as Carl and the boys carried the old washer from behind the cabins and set it on the cement platform next to the white electric washer and the hot water pipe.

"I think she'll hold water," Carl said.

"I'll get the metal tubs!" I offered. dragging two heavy basins from the side of the bathhouse.

Carl filled the wooden tubs with hot water. We watched the bottom of the wooden machine.

"No leaks!" Carl yelled.

Rocky and Terry cheered.

"This is going to be fun," I said clapping my hands. "Just like the old days!"

Mom stood there silent, frowning. I knew she wasn't convinced the ancient appliance would save the day because she was staring at it like she did the maggots: *the wretched debris of a bygone era—someone's cast-offs*. I don't think she saw anything fun about any of it.

The boys gathered up laundry and carried it to the washer. I wondered if the rusted hand wringer could manage the heavy blankets.

Carl handed me an old broom handle. "You propel the sheets into a tumbling motion. One side for washing, one side for rinsing." I grinned and pulled the broom handle through the water. Soap suds foamed up and over the sides.

After some time Carl guided a sheet corner through the wobbly wringer and turned the crank. Mom stepped closer. The crank squeaked as the sheet rolled out the other side of the wringer;

Mom grabbed it. She guided the sheet into the metal tub and the sheet collapsed onto the bottom of the tub and folded onto itself, over and over. Mom and I carried the first tub of clean clothes to the clotheslines together. Over the next several days Mom and I washed clothes.

While we waited for the clothes to dry we helped Carl and the boys clean the pools with shovels and putty knives. We scraped red and brown algae scum from the sides and bottom of the swimming pool, beginning at the shallow end, inch by inch, working our way down the slanted cement to the deep end. The more we scraped, the more there was to do. We shoveled the jelly-like junk into buckets and carried it away. Bucket after bucket was filled, emptied, and refilled—such a dirty, discouraging job. Everyone looked forward to a bath.

Only when clean linens were fitted to the army cots in the bedrooms, fresh towels were folded in stacks in the laundry room and we finished our baths did we gather up our things from the cabins and carry them to the Lodge. We couldn't wait until the swimming pool refilled with clean, warm water. And we felt so proud, knowing we had the biggest bathtubs in the whole world.

I was delighted with my new room across the hall from Mom and Carl's room although disappointed I didn't have a closet like my old room in town. My parents' room had the biggest window and the only closet in the valley, probably the only closet between the Springs and Fairbanks. The boys shared a bedroom. The fourth room was going to be the guest room.

"I'll make you a closet, Gwennie, a real nice one," Carl said.

The passing of June convinced the cow moose Carl had named Lucy that the valley was still a refuge of safety. She strolled in for meals of clover almost every evening. She always brought her baby calf now. We named the calf Molly, and she grew fast. From one visit to the next I measured her growth by a tree limb near the hot water pools that I could see from the Lodge, where she always stood and grazed.

When June was nearly gone we bleached the wooden mats and moldy benches in the bathhouse, then returned them to the bathing areas. Carl began to repair the walls in the bathhouse and replace chinking between the logs in the Lodge. By the time Carl and the boys had most of the saggy ceilings mended, I had secured permission to paint the shelves in the pantry. Rocky and Terry painted the washstands in all six cabins using the same green paint. Mom found enough water dippers to put one in each cabin near a water bucket and soap dish.

That's when I started getting twinges in my stomach, thinking about waiting tables on the Fourth of July. When I helped Mom put clean towels in the cabins she went over the list of dos and don'ts again, about serving the guests. The conversations were comforting and encouraging but the words did not take away the knots in my tummy.

The boys and I went swimming every evening. One evening on our way to the pool, Carl told the boys he had found a spot up the airfield for a dumpsite. The next morning he cranked up the little Oliver. It coughed and sputtered from the stable all the way to the rear of the Lodge.

"Now you boys take turns, you hear?" Carl said as he hitched the trailer to the rear of the little tractor.

Rocky drove the little Cat up the airfield to the dumpsite and Terry drove it back down. This routine continued for the better part of the day until it dawned on Terry that he was always towing an empty trailer—boring.

I carried the garbage from the kitchen out to the junk pile when they were putting another load into the trailer, and arguing over who was going to drive the Oliver back up the airfield to the dumpsite.

"It's not fair," Terry said.

"That's just the way it worked out. What's the big deal, anyway? You get to drive the little Cat, don't you?" said Rocky.

"If it's not a big deal, why don't you haul the trailer with nothing in it?" Terry asked.

The lodge looked much like this when the Wilsons arrived and when they left. They added the bird cage for "Tweety Bird." The door behind the bird cage goes into the dining room and kitchen. The door to the left, into the bedrooms. Many cords of wood were burned in the old barrel stove.

"Carl said we're supposed to take turns. If you drive now, you get more turns than me."

"I want to haul the junk," Terry said, throwing an armload of trash into the trailer, then turning to face Rocky. If I can't haul the junk, too, I'm telling Carl on you."

"Okay, you drive."

Terry pulled his cowboy hat down partway over his eyes and climbed up on the Oliver. Rocky climbed into the trailer. The boys proceeded up the airfield with a loaded trailer, with Terry driving and looking back over his shoulder at Rocky, slouched in a corner of the trailer among the junk. For two more days the boys hauled junk. I knew Terry had never told Carl about their argument because if he had Carl would have put a stop to the whole operation.

Thursday afternoon before the weekend of the Fourth, Chuck brought mail and supplies. "There are enough reservations to fill the cabins," Carl said to Chuck, grinning, "and we can count on more people to fly in just to swim and eat. Help me move the ping-pong table into the dining room, Chuck. That way we can serve more people at one time. I'll shorten the legs in the morning."

That evening after Chuck left, we took the fishing trip and picnic Carl promised at the West Fork on the old trail, five miles below the Springs. The break was a joyous time for all of us, complete with hot dogs and marshmallows, a little fishing, rock-skimming, and tours through the old remains of an early roadhouse nearby, one which had slept and fed many travelers from Fairbanks to the Hot Springs in years past.

The boys and I didn't find many forgotten possessions worth keeping hidden beneath the rotting logs. I did find an area that I guessed was once the kitchen, though, where broken cups and plates had at one time rested on a shelf. I left the ruins, and walked slowly along the gravel bar of the West Fork to return to our campfire. A good distance ahead of me, in the gravel near the water's edge, a spot on the gravel bar came into view with what looked like yellow rocks leaping like Mexican jumping beans.

I couldn't figure out what I was seeing, I was so far away. Maybe I wasn't seeing clearly, or the late evening sun rays were coming through the trees, dancing on the edge of the creek. I continued walking and the image changed as I watched.

The jumping rocks were not rocks, but butterflies! Yellow and black Swallowtails fluttered their wings as they lighted on the rocks damp with creek water from earlier, when we had skipped rocks across the creek. There were loads of butterflies—too many to count. I stood there spellbound beyond belief, wondering what in the world they thought they were doing. Butterflies don't fly in flocks; they fly alone, free and beautiful. I walked closer, and away they flew, each butterfly in a different direction, higher and higher toward the cloudless evening sky until I could no longer see them.

The picnic at the West Fork turned out to be a day I would remember for a very long time. When I went to bed that night, the doubts that had bothered me for weeks concerning the grand opening on the Fourth seemed to have gone away. I no longer felt any twinges in my tummy about waiting tables for a dining room full of strangers. Somehow after swirling for days, those fears had scattered, flying away beyond my mind's view, and in the morning, they were still gone.

CHAPTER 16

Fourth of July, 1954

———

Friday, at twenty past ten o'clock in the morning, Fairbanks Air Service rumbled down the runway in a monstrous tubby bumblebee called a twin Cessna. The morning sun was warmer than usual and a fire in the wood range made for a hot kitchen. I watched from the window, absorbed in the vision of the antiquated black and yellow plane.

Carl shook hands with the pilot. Two rough-looking men slung backpacks and gear from inside the plane to the side of the airfield. The pilot unloaded the groceries.

"They'd better have sent everything," I heard Mom say under her breath as Carl and the men stacked cases of food onto the kitchen floor. Introductions were made amidst the aroma of bread baking. Hawley Evans, tall, with lots of curly dark hair and the owner of Fairbanks Air Service said he was going back for another load and guests. I thought I saw a small dimple in one cheek.

Jim Stanley was a large man with big, worn-out boots. A rumpled brimmed hat flopped over pale blue eyes that squinted. He was missing some teeth. Byron Johnson said to please call him "Red," because everybody did in view of the fact that his hair was red. Red was shorter than Jim, much thinner, and wore a black porkpie hat much like the one stuck full of fish hooks that I hung up outside the cabin near the North Fork. He talked exactly like the people in movies who live in the South.

Overview of the Chena Hot Springs grounds showing the new covered building over the swimming pool just over the top of the airplane wing. The new log building on the right, built by Carl and his crew, was used mainly for food storage. The large smoke stack is from the army cook stove in the kitchen. (Henry Kaiser collection.)

Hawley made a hasty exit out the back door, grumbling about a bumpy runway with too many rocks. Carl led Jim and Red to the main room of the Lodge. Mom shoved leftovers around in the cooler to make room for salad dressings and olives. I grabbed as many egg cartons as I could carry and trailed after the men in a businesslike manner all the way to the cellar. I didn't want to miss a word, just in case anything was said about George Wilson or his friend Gregg.

Red drawled on about trapping, fishing, and hunting as I descended the steps into the cellar. I had trouble handling both the flashlight and the eggs because my curiosity was busy paying attention to their conversation. Jim said he was going to walk down to Gregg's old place. I set the eggs down, climbed out of the cellar and stood quietly by the bar.

"Going to spend a week or so at Gregg's old place before opening up my cabin at the North Fork," Jim explained.

I thought for sure Carl would ask some questions about Gregg, or George Wilson, but he didn't. Red and Jim left the Lodge shortly afterwards, retrieved their gear from the side of the airfield and headed down the trail on foot.

Still, for me to meet Jim Stanley was really something because he had known both Gregg and George Wilson, which brought them a notch closer to reality than when they were just characters in the stories Carl told.

The rest of the morning was like getting ready for a big party. Carl cranked up the generator as the guests would arrive at any time. I arranged candy bars and chewing gum on the bar counter next to the old ledgers that bestowed what I thought was significant flair for an old roadhouse. Carl stacked beer and soda pop beside the tomatoes and lettuce Hawley had brought that morning in the little refrigerator under the bar, while Mom made final preparations for the evening meal.

I took a quick bath. Carl was cutting off the legs of the ping-pong table. When I returned from the bathhouse Mom was scrubbing a shorter table.

"When I get through here I'll take my bath, Gwennie. Get dressed and start peeling potatoes," Mom said.

When Mom returned from her bath I was still in my bedroom fussing with my two ugly pigtails. She told me to get to the kitchen. I peeled potatoes until I was almost sick of it.

"That's too thick," she kept saying. "Don't peel it all away, Gwennie." She mixed up a cake, every few minutes dabbing sweat from her forehead then tucking the Kleenex back under the belt of her dress.

Hawley made two more trips before I had the tables set for dinner. More planes arrived and although I was disappointed not to learn anything new about George from those two old-timers, I was looking forward to the time of my life, with the Lodge full of guests. I iced the chocolate cake.

As the guests arrived, Carl asked each of them to sign the old ledger: Russ Williams, Randy and Marian Acord, Jeff Studdert, and a very old man named Max Reedy who was from Fox, ten miles north of Fairbanks, who had trouble walking. Max had operated a general merchandise store in Fox since the early days. Now he wanted to rent one of the old cabins for two weeks so he could soak in the hot water for his "doggone rheumatism."

Two mean-looking bulldogs with long, pink tongues hanging out of their mouths belonged to Randy Acord. The dogs took to charging across the meadow to the side hill on the other side of Spring Creek. A lady and her husband, Tom, took the first cabin. Burt Collins flew in after the swallows lined up on the wires to the Lodge. Before the evening sunlight danced on the kitchen counters, nine planes were tied down in a row on the runway. I kept track of time by the activities at the resort.

The next morning I stumbled into the kitchen at 5 A.M. The wood range was already crackling. Mom had cookie sheets lined with bacon slices ready for the oven. She was carrying on in a way I had never seen her act before.

"Everyone will start coming in here and we still have to set the table. Gwen, get cereal ready, and milk, and syrup. Better fix four butter dishes. Put jam and jelly on the table. Somebody might want molasses. Put that on, too," Mom said, her face red and her tone businesslike. Her list was endless.

I piled little boxes of cold cereal in a large bowl, mixed canned peaches and pears in another bowl, and set the tables. I filled pitchers with the syrup we had made the week before. Carl started frying pancakes on three black stovetop griddles. Mom called everyone to breakfast and returned to the kitchen.

Mom yelled at me in a whisper, "Gwennie, help crack eggs for the big, black frying pan."

After breakfast most of the men walked to the North Fork to fish for grayling. Those who didn't go fishing napped, or went for a swim, or had a big lunch of homemade soup, sandwiches, potato and macaroni salads.

Shortly before noon Mom let out a yelp: "The dinner rolls!" With breakfast, dishes, and preparing lunch, the rolls for the evening meal had slipped her mind. She grabbed a large bowl, poured out flour, mixed yeast and sugar together and measured water while I greased three pans.

Rocky and Terry chopped wood. All afternoon the cast iron range gobbled up wood in preparation for the evening meal and drained the firewood box empty several times. Carl had set up a chopping stump behind the kitchen and, like his funny toy red bird that dunked its ugly head in a small bowl of water endlessly, the boys kept chopping and chopping, stacking the wood box as high as they could get it.

"Take some of that wood out. It's going to fall over," Mom said.

Just before dinner Mom's hairdo turned into a wringing mop of limp, no-curl mess. The kitchen was suffocating; opening the windows had not made much difference. More people flew in. Carl turned people away because there was no place for them to sleep and the count for dinner increased. Mom was a nervous wreck.

Then, loaded down with backpacks and worn duffle bags, Shorty Harbell and Smitty Smith arrived. They were spending the holiday at Sully's cabin on the North Fork. They shuffled past the kitchen windows from the airfield towards the front door of the Lodge in lace-up rubber boots, faded black trousers and rumpled tan shirts. Meanwhile, tin cups and buckets clanged against the buckles on their worn-out gear like old prospectors I had seen in magazines.

By the time dinner was ready to serve Mom had calmed down. The guests entered the dining room and I watched Mom greet each one with the poise and warmth with which I was familiar. Mom and I were exhausted. I stood at the kitchen sink, feeling quite grownup in my yellow skirt and matching blouse. I wore a wrinkle-free apron, one of several Grandma Heller had made long ago, tied in a big bow around my waist.

"Remember, when they come in for dinner and sit down, don't forget to ask if they want coffee," Mom said.

This Fourth of July teemed with exciting new experiences for me, yet pouring coffee by myself had not been one of the happier ones. The thought of doing it made my stomach churn. Distrust of myself began to surface and I felt like a little girl again.

"And smile!" Mom added. "You might get another tip. I need to go and fix my hair." With all the activity and the heat of the stove, her cheeks were now as red as her nylon dress.

"Be courteous," she had told me. "Ask if they need anything, pour coffee from the right side, remove cups from the table before pouring. Take dirty dishes away from the left side and never, never, reach over anyone's plate."

The plan was for her to slip in the front door of the Lodge while everyone was in the dining room, dash into her bedroom, fix her hair while the guests ate, then sneak back to the kitchen before anyone noticed she had left.

Mom scurried out the back door of the kitchen and around the corner of the building for her bedroom. The dos and don'ts of pouring coffee jumbled up in my head. Silverware clinked in the dining room.

Chuck Gray was a friend of Carl's before our family went to the Springs. His main vocation was working at the local newspaper but he had a side job as a big game guide. His flying ability proved an asset to us at the Springs.

I picked at what was left of the baked ham on the cutting board and watched the back door for Mom's return. Was there enough time for her to get back before anyone wanted coffee?

Pies cooled on the counter. I had rolled out the dough myself. If anyone asked, I wasn't to tell anyone where the apples came from because they might not eat them if they knew they were canned.

It was too much to remember. I ate another piece of ham. What if I dropped the pot? What if I spilled coffee or made a mess *and* burned someone? I crossed fingers on both hands but Mom still did not return. I heard Carl laugh again from the main room. I took a deep breath, forced a big smile, grabbed the coffee pot and walked into the dining room.

"Coffee?" I said in a little voice that didn't sound like my usual one. The ping-pong table sat twelve: two places on each end and five on the sides. The smaller table sat eight. Everyone stared at me.

"Yes, please," smiled a large woman sitting at the far end of the ping-pong table near the window. I thought *I'm not going to be able to squeeze behind her chair.*

"This is great," said Tom, who had rented the first cabin. "You tell your mother this is the most food I've seen in some time!"

I filled Tom's cup. My hands shook as I made my way to the window and filled the big lady's cup, and I smiled, but I felt the corners of my mouth quivering.

"Did you cook this all by yourself?" the lady asked sweetly. Her hair was still wet from the pool and her perfume stunk. She grinned at me.

I cleared my throat, "Well, I helped." My cheeks grew hot as the serving dishes appeared to float around the table. I stepped to the next person, Tom's wife.

"You look very pretty. How grown-up, to help your Mother the way you do," Tom's wife said.

"Coffee?" I squeaked. Tom's wife nodded. "Don't you miss not being able to play with your friends?" I swallowed and shook my head no.

The two bulldogs had planted themselves at the other end of the table. They panted, their eyes watching everything through slots. White bubbly froth dripped from their pink tongues and pooled into puddles on the floor I had mopped earlier that week.

I poured coffee like I was watching a movie. Bowls seemed to float and the guests' voices seemed far away. I crept around the dogs. I refilled butter dishes and jelly bowls. Whenever I could, I glanced into the kitchen hoping to see Mom. I poured more water and when all twenty guests had been politely asked if they cared for or didn't care for anything else, I headed for the safety of the hot kitchen.

With one ear tuned to the dining room, the other listening for footsteps on the back porch, I heard Carl laugh again and in walked

Mom. She had a fresh hairdo, but her face was still flushed deep red. I wanted to say something.

"Did you get the coffee in there?" she asked anxiously.

"Yes! But everybody keeps staring at me! How come you didn't come back?"

"Did it taste okay?"

"I kept watching for you. What took you so long?"

"Did they like the dinner?"

"Everybody said they did. I don't like those dogs."

We cut three apple pies and part of a fourth. Still, no one asked about the apples or knew they were eating on a sawed-off ping-pong table.

"See if anyone else wants more coffee," Mom said.

"They don't want any more," I sighed.

"Gwendolyn!"

I collected $3.20 in tips when I cleared the table. Mom retrieved an empty peanut butter jar from the pantry.

"By the end of the summer you'll have enough saved up to buy something special for school, Gwennie," Mom assured me, placing the tip money inside the jar and setting it on the top shelf next to the cookbooks. I felt sad and thought it very strange to feel blue when there was nothing to feel sad about.

"You did a very nice job, Gwennie." Mom gave me a tight hug.

By nine o'clock the last plane had taxied up the airfield to take off for Fairbanks. The freedom of isolation and silence once again blanketed the small valley. Rocky and Terry made a mad dash for the swimming pool. They screeched for joy, skinny legs swishing in oversized swim trunks, their swim-towels flapping from bare backs like Superman's cape.

The same feeling of sadness I had felt earlier pushed its way into my throat. I thought I was going to cry.

Mom and I finished up a mountain of dirty dishes. Carl helped wash, whistling. Later Carl and Mom relaxed in the empty Lodge with a cup of coffee. I walked through on my way to the pool, clad in a white swimsuit, with a swim cap pulled tight around my ears.

"Just imagine, Belle!" I heard Carl say. "We'd have more people here if we had enough cabins for them to stay in." I sat on a chair and listened. "...and more for dinner, if the dining room were bigger," Carl added as he rose from the couch, walked to the small window beside the bar and gazed out at the swimming pool.

I heard the boys scream as they jumped into the water.

"If the pool had a roof on it, we could use it in the winter," Carl said. He turned from the window and grinned at Mom. "This place could be big again...as big as it was in the early days." His face shimmered.

I felt his pioneering spirit as he talked of building cabins, restoring the old sawmill against the hill along Spring Creek, knocking out a wall to extend the dining room, and grading the old trail so he could drive fishermen to the North Fork and the West Fork.

"Well? What do you think?" he asked Mom, now speaking to her more slowly.

I looked at Mom. She did not look excited. "I don't think I could handle many more people than what we had this weekend, Carl."

"Oh! Well, you won't have to. We'll hire a cook—think of it."

Mom looked interested now.

"With a little more work we could build this place into something really nice. Let's take a walk up the airfield."

I walked to the pool and stepped down into the shallow end. With my back against the rough cement wall, I watched my brothers play. None of us knew how to swim yet, so we didn't venture near the deep end. It was no more than five feet deep but well over our heads and scary. Carl promised to teach us to swim by the end of summer.

The boys pretended to drown one another, splashed water at each other, held their noses and took turns dropping underwater until the other one screamed. *Boys,* I thought.

The warm water slapped at my neck as I thought of how Carl had shared his ideas with such happiness. I envisioned cabins encircling the Hot Springs, with bathrooms, matching bedspreads and new furniture, and an enormous dining room with lots of tables for four covered with colorful tablecloths. There could even be pictures on the walls. I could wear a uniform like the waitresses at the Model Café and carry a little book to write down orders. Mom could pour the coffee because we would have a cook. I wished we could stay at the Springs forever.

I waded out towards the deep end of the pool wanting not to return to Fairbanks for school. Summer was not going to last much longer and that made me feel very sad. Terry splashed my face with water. I splashed him back. Rocky splashed both of us and the water fight was on.

───────

It was the middle of July before we saw Jim and Red again. They walked up the trail for a bath. I had been so anxious for them to return. They couldn't go back to town without my knowing about it. The only way out was for them to walk back to the Springs and fly back to town. Carl invited them to stay for stew.

The conversations over dinner were full of stories about the "old days" and how times weren't what they used to be and how life used to be more fun without all the fancy machines that made the days complicated and tougher. I wanted to ask Jim about Gregg. I was trying very hard to get up enough nerve to ask him when Carl brought the subject up. "Tell me what you remember about ol' Gregg and the early days here at the Springs," Carl said.

"Well, I seen 'em come and I seen 'em go, Boy," Jim said, sopping up gravy from his dinner plate with a chunk of bread. "Nobody ever stayed here long enough to make a go of it 'cept George Wilson, winters too hard and too long." Gregg made his headquarters at his North Fork cabin then, about ten miles below the Springs. This place was boomin'."

"When did Gregg first come here?" asked Carl.

Carl is on the D4, Terry on the Oliver tractor and Rocky with Totem. All worked to clean up soon after their arrival. Note the large pole propping up the front gable of the Lodge. Carl soon found a more esthetic way to support the logs.

Jim slid his plate to the side and reached into a shirt pocket for a toothpick. "Fall of nineteen and ought seven, he told me. Said the only thing here was the old bathhouse them first guys built. It stood too long, was rotten. Gregg called it *gnarly*. It was when George filed on the homestead that Gregg started comin' up to the Springs every month with another fella name of Floyd Blankenship. The two of 'em boasted to everyone about knowing the country on the Upper Chena. They built a roadhouse and prospected. Loggin' was Gregg's principal holdout and he did a lot of that; they floated them clear to Fairbanks, to the mill."

Mom rose to clear the dishes. I had barely touched my supper. Rocky and Terry sat quietly, waiting for cake.

Jim went on. "They hunted moose and caribou every fall; that old rock house is still up there where they waited for herds of caribou to pass through back on them ridges."

Red said little during all of this. I was sure Jim's story was a new one to Red. Carl only interrupted Jim a couple of times.

Jim leaned back in his chair. "See, Blankenship's theory was a volcano was here once, and the soil is the off-falls. Gregg said it reminded Blankenship of his father's farm near Wenatchee where he

171

grew up. Gregg said there were better growin' conditions here than he had ever seen in Eastern Washington. They bought cabbages, taters, rutabagas, and turnips from George and packed 'em twelve miles down to the cabin.

"Gregg said travelers didn't quit comin', that George had to keep an eye out for fires and illegal wood-cuttin' most days. That's when George got the idea to put up a new bathhouse, a bigger one. George wanted to build small cabins, too, for people who came along, and charge them a fee, invest the money into cultivating the land for growing crops and then sell the vegetables. Blankenship even worked for George some—cleared land and hauled logs."

For the rest of July, every weekend was a busy one for our family. There was little rain. Weekdays were spent getting ready for weekends. Carl's greatest concern was still the condition of the grounds, the outbuildings, and the interior of the Lodge. He always had new projects for the boys and me, which left hardly any time for play. Chuck flew up after work with the mail once a week. He always stayed to swim and ended up teaching us kids to swim. Hawley delivered meat, eggs and fresh produce for the weekend and it was my job to sweep out the Lodge every Friday morning.

One afternoon in August, Shorty Harbell walked up from the North Fork. The thermometer outside the dining room window had stayed near eighty degrees most of the week and one day when the sun was high Shorty shuffled up the trail from Sully's cabin for a cup of tea and a bath.

Mondays were washdays. We were now washing clothes in the kitchen and hanging them out behind the Lodge to dry. On this particular day Carl had pulled up to the back door of the Lodge in the jeep as I walked up from the cabins carrying a load of dirty sheets. He shut off the engine and climbed out of the jeep as Shorty met him.

"How you doing, Shorty?" Carl asked.

"Just fine, Sir." He took off his hat.

"Look what I found," Carl said, pointing to the back seat.

"Ice?" asked Shorty. He ran a gnarled hand across a large chunk of ice and chuckled. He was barely five feet tall, in his mid-sixties, with blue eyes that twinkled like the eyes of an elf.

"Yup," Carl said. "Found it under the moss at the other end of the airfield. Have you ever seen clearer ice than this? Crystal clear! Not a speck of dirt in any of it." He lifted out a chunk and carried it to the back door.

The boys were chopping wood. Every weekend they looked forward to Mondays so they could chop and haul wood with the little Oliver tractor. Carl hollered to them to give him a hand. I took the bedding to the laundry room.

Carl never charged Shorty for baths. Shorty had spent most of his life in the United States so his speech seldom reflected his homeland. Every now and then his Irish brogue and mannerisms showed his polished upbringing. I looked forward to his visits; he was teaching me to play cribbage.

Shorty was inspecting the ice when I returned. Carl asked if Walt was going to town over the weekend. Without looking up, Shorty said, "He is. Suppose to be retired. Ha! Since he left the Model Café, he's busier than ever cookin' for those big shindigs in town."

"Smitty coming back up?" asked Carl.

"He is," Shorty said, watching the boys chop up the ice.

"Trading weekends at the cabin with Smitty seems to work pretty well, doesn't it? Walt told me Smitty used to be a darn good cook, too. Said he used to cook up at Deadwood and a few other mining camps around."

"Yes Sir, works very well, but those two will put pounds on me, if I don't watch it. Guess I'll be takin' me bath now, if it's okay with you," Shorty said.

"Sure. We're going to make ice cream. Maybe Max wants to come over," Carl said.

Shorty smiled. He replaced his hat and walked to the bathhouse.

Today was a real treat. Carl and the boys gathered up ingredients to make the ice cream. The boys had only managed two trips to Monument Creek to fish this summer. Aside from the picnic at the West Fork, playing cowboys and Indians, and chasing Topsey and Holly, we had worked. Mom prepared a cup of tea and gingerbread. Max Reedy was waiting for Shorty when he came from his bath.

Carl dished up ice cream while Shorty sat with Max, exchanging tales of Alaska—stories of life in the mining camps before there were cars. Shorty rarely talked about where he was from. He poured some tea into his saucer then sipped it from there. The clicking of his false teeth made me want to laugh aloud.

Before he left for his cabin, Shorty lingered outside in front of the Lodge under a setting sun. "I never seen so many fish like I seen this summer. Caught so many I built me a cold box so I can keep the fish alive in the North Fork until I want to eat one," Shorty said as he swatted at a bee buzzing near his head. The bee wouldn't leave. The more Shorty talked, the more the bee buzzed around him, till he went and landed on the end of Shorty's nose.

Mom's expression seemed to say *don't let on like you see it*. The boys choked down laughter.

I saw Carl grin and thought he was going to say something about it, but he didn't.

I was afraid the bee would sting Shorty right there on the end of his nose. I watched as the bee rubbed its back legs together and flicked its wings up and down.

"Thanks for the tea, folks, and the ice cream!" Shorty stated firmly, putting on his hat as he told Max he'd see him tomorrow. He gave a slight nod of his head and shuffled back down the trail with the bee crisscrossing behind him, never knowing how close he had come to a painful parting.

By the end of the week Max Reedy had flown back to town. During the month he was at the Springs, Max had set himself a strict regimen of two, sometimes three, baths a day. Max's routine successfully relieved the pain in his muscles and joints. Max left for town with a bounce in his step instead of a limp. *A real miracle*, I thought.

It wasn't long before Jack Frost began to pay us visits during the night. Days grew shorter as we neared the first of September. The robins and swallows knew how close winter was. I'd watched their numbers thin daily, and regiments of water fowl spanned the cloud-dotted sky in V-formation, honking their way south. The sun hid its face behind the hill earlier every afternoon and as the hillside above Spring Creek turned yellow, red and orange, the boys and I discussed the coming winter while playing in the swimming pool. The time had come when we had to go back to town.

For me to find even one good reason to go back to town for school was useless. The boys said they would miss not being able to drive the Oliver tractor. Each day the patterns of silver frost spread, and each morning the windows awoke etched with white woodland scenes. Jack Frost no longer felt like my friend.

Several mornings later breakfast passed in almost complete silence, with only an occasional clink of silverware. Carl didn't joke about it. I knew why. Our wonderful summer was coming to an end.

CHAPTER 17

Ravens

Before the cold and snow set in, many of the birds would leave the valley, except of course the ravens and the chickadees. I viewed the ravens of the valley as the lucky ones, lucky because they didn't have to fly south when winter came. Winter was approaching faster than ravens could fly. Air traffic would halt after Labor Day. What a sad thought.

"The raven is tough, through ice, snow—through the coldest temperatures. This is his land and the raven will stay the winter," Carl said to no one in particular that morning at breakfast. He stared out the dining room window, his elbows on the table as if watching a sad movie.

Of the many birds at the Hot Springs, the chickadee was the smallest. It seemed to me the chickadees, rather than the larger birds, should be the ones to look for warmer homes in the cold weather. I also decided the only reason the chickadees stayed was so the ravens would have someone to boss around all winter.

"I've been thinking about staying the winter at the Springs," Carl said.

A clump of chewed pancakes lodged in my throat and I started coughing.

"Yea," Terry squealed, making circles in the air with his fork.

Carl said, "With the leave of absence from the Lathrop Company, what better time to make major repairs? Visitor traffic will be next to nothing. That will give me time to do the heavy work that needs to be done."

"Yeah," Rocky said, dripping honey on his pancakes and nodded his head like a grown-up.

Secretly I'd wished many times we could stay at the Springs forever. All my wishes with the chicken bones were for us not to go back to town. I knew wishes couldn't really come true; Mom hung wishbones behind the stove in the kitchen to dry. The boys and I drew straws to see who got to make a wish.

"It's a perfect time," Carl went on. "I can put a roof over the swimming pool, replace rotten logs in the bathhouse and work on the trail, maybe even start a walkway from the Lodge to the pool this fall before it snows."

My wishes had come true. The Springs was going to be our very own home forever. I happily envisioned the coming of winter. Going back to town was an idea I didn't have to think about anymore. But now there was something else for me to think about. What about school? What were we going to do about school?

"What's a 'leaf of abscess?'" asked Terry.

Mom threw Carl a scowl, a look I had never seen her aim at him. Something was up.

"You kids have to go back to town with your mother after Labor Day like we talked about."

Mom left the table. The boys stared at their empty plates. It was so quiet in the dining room I could hear the rushing water over in Monument Creek on the other side of the airfield. How could we leave Carl all alone with the ravens?

On August 20th hunting season opened. Temperatures called for light jackets or sweaters, and Carl planned a moose hunt. I had always envisioned my first year in junior high school as something wonderful because seventh grade meant being a big kid and being a big kid meant walking to the big gray school building facing Cushman Street. All the high school kids went to Main School, too. I had looked forward to this for a long time. Now, I was all mixed up. While Carl and the boys were away hunting I mustered up enough courage to ask Mom about the town situation.

"There is something good to be found in everything, Gwennie," Mom said gently. "If we must return to town, we must. Whatever your dad decides to do is what must be done." As hard as I tried, I found nothing good in any of it. What troubled me the most was that we always had to do what Carl said.

Carl and the boys returned from hunting in two days. Carl nailed a massive moose rack to the wall in the Lodge over the door of the dining room. With a puffed-out chest, he stood back and gazed upon the animal's fighting equipment. Nights turned colder. I helped Carl chop the moose into usable-size pieces without much conversation between the two of us. I brooded most of that week about town and school, about Carl staying in one place and the rest of our family in another.

Late Friday afternoon, walloping raps above the Lodge sent me racing out the back door of the kitchen. A crowd of ravens lurked behind the kitchen. I yelled at them. "Go away. I'm tougher than you are." The ravens, first with one eye, then the other, peered at me for only a second, then put their beaks to poking the ground for food. They strutted back and forth in front of me with their feathers all puffed out.

"Shoo!" I yelled again.

Far above the birds, a helicopter circled the valley three times, like some huge dragonfly, before descending. The air smelled metal like snow. I watched the ravens lift to the sky with slow, determined wing flaps, squawking one at a time as the helicopter touched ground near the lower end of the field. I rushed back to the kitchen, through the dining room and into the Lodge. Gasping at the air, I blurted, "There's an army helicopter out there." I ran to the window by the bar and looked out. "Two army guys are coming in."

Carl promptly left through the front door and waited on the dirt path for the men to approach the Lodge. From inside, Mom and the boys and I watched the officers march toward Carl. The tall man clutched a clipboard, and the short man carried a briefcase. Silver and gold medals sparkled from their dark green military flight jackets while the long scarves looped around their furry collars flapped in the wind. Hats sat square on their heads and round, black sunglasses hid their eyes.

Carl shook hands with the men. The man with the briefcase started talking and pointing to the upper end of the airfield and then to the hill above Spring Creek. The hillside was viv-

A determined Carl Wilson discusses the improvements he has made in the property and the ones he hopes to make with a photographer, barely visible on the left.

id with color patterns resembling the handmade quilt Mom had saved and draped over the back of an old rocking chair in the first old cabin. I believed she had stitched the quilt from skirts worn by ladies who had lived in the valley once.

Carl led the men inside the bathhouse.

"What do they want?" asked Rocky.

"I have no idea. But I hope they don't want anything to eat," Mom said.

"It has to do with airplanes. There must be something going on in these hills," I said.

"The Russians are coming," Terry said.

Across the clearing at Spring Creek near the base of the hill and the hot water, Carl and the men talked some more. When they entered the Lodge the man with the clipboard asked Mom if they could see the dining room. His eyes scanned the dining room without the slightest turn of his head. "How many can you serve at one time?" he asked Mom. "Some will want meals, at least one meal a day. Is it possible to have several settings?"

180

Mom smiled, glanced quickly at Carl and said, "Oh, sure."

The other man opened his briefcase and shuffled through some papers. "A hundred men are scheduled to hike from Eielson Air Force Base into Chena Hot Springs on maneuvers with Col. Greer before the snow flies in September," he said, handing some papers to Carl.

Mom smiled again.

"This will be payday for the Springs. The boys will have plenty of money to spend and believe you me they'll spend it. Most will want hot baths and a swim."

They wanted the bar opened. Carl said okay. They wanted permission to play cards. Carl nodded.

Two nights later Carl was washing up for supper at the kitchen sink. The boys had gone for wood, a chore they now complained about every night.

"Your mom and I have been thinking about you kids having school at the Springs this winter," he said.

I looked at Mom. She stirred the thick off-white gravy without looking up. Carl dried his hands, folded the towel and draped the towel on the edge of the sink. He leaned against the sink and folded his arms across his chest, his eyes somewhat bigger than slits.

I knew he was waiting for me to respond. However much I wanted what he said to be true, something inside me said it would never come true. Lately what he said and what happened did not always match. I did not respond.

I took dinner plates off the shelf and set them on the counter. I looked to Mom for a nod, a smile, a frown, a no-teeth smile, anything to confirm or deny Carl's statement. I circled the top plate with five glasses and counted out silverware and carried it all into the dining room. I began setting the table for supper. Who would be our teacher? Where would we get books? School at the Springs? How was that even possible? It probably wasn't, I decided.

I returned to the kitchen just as the back door flew open. Rocky and Terry stomped inside, carrying firewood stacked in their arms, up to their noses. They heaved sticks of split wood into the wood box, grumbling about how cold it was outside. I thought about telling them what Carl had said, but instead I clutched my teeth firmly so I couldn't talk.

"Don't forget to close that door, Rocky," Mom said.

Mom poured the gravy into a blue bowl and mashed the potatoes. The boys left, slamming the back door on the way out. Mom added canned milk a little at a time until the potatoes fluffed into little mountains.

"We could hire a teacher," Carl said watching me. "She'd stay in one of the old cabins. We'll make another cabin into a school house. Mom flopped big spoonsful of creamy mashed potatoes into a round serving dish, cut a square of butter, poked it firmly into the center of the potato mound and tapped several times on the can of paprika, dusting the potato pile with brick red.

Terry marched through the kitchen into the dining room with more wood, Rocky right behind him. Mom handed me the potatoes and flashed me a no-teeth smile as if to say this is our secret for now.

⌒

Fifteen airplanes parked at the lower end of the runway on Labor Day Monday. The long weekend had been so much bigger than the Fourth of July that Carl had to turn people away again, as we were full up. My jar of tips mounted to well above the half-full mark. One man left a silver dollar.

I spoke to the boys about having school at the Springs. They didn't have much to say, but it was all I could think about. I wouldn't get to walk to the Fairbanks public school on Cushman Street but I decided that home-schooling at the Hot Springs had to be much more exciting.

Chuck flew in later that day with his parents and brought the mail. They stayed for the evening meal and before they left Carl read us a letter from Baltimore. The letter had come in the mail that day.

Gwen serves drinks to a guest, Bernice Gray, and Gwen's mother on a summer afternoon near the large garden in the background.

"The Territory of Alaska provides education through a correspondence course in Baltimore, Maryland. The Calvert Course will supply all books, school materials, lesson guides and teacher manuals for each grade," Carl read. "A Calvert teacher in Baltimore has been assigned to each student and necessary supplies along with teaching instructions for Mrs. Wilson have been shipped and should arrive soon."

"Looks like we won't need to hire that teacher, Gwennie," said Carl.

"Geez," Rocky said. "Stay here and go to school? You can show me how to build a trapline like Shorty told us about."

"Yeah, me, too," Terry said.

I threw my arms around Carl and gave him a hug. I was as tough as the ravens. We could make this new arrangement work.

Carl said, "We'd better go to town this next weekend, Belle. Chuck said he'd return on Saturday."

Saturday arrived and Chuck's Cessna lifted us off the airfield like a bird. We zoomed over Sully's cabin on the North Fork and banked against the Big Hill, climbing above the land and its river, until the earth looked like a new and mysterious planet. I thought of George Wilson discovering the Springs and what it was like for the Swans, poling up the river winding below us like a long, gray ribbon. I thought *now we're the ones making a trip to town.*

The house in town rented quickly. Joanne Bachner came over and stood watching Aunt Pat help Mom pack. Pat emptied all the cupboards and crated dishes. I was helping Carl pack old books in big cardboard barrels in the basement when Joanne told me her dad knew somebody who had a dog that needed a home. They thought the woods where we live now would be perfect.

In the afternoon Carl and I went to pick up our order at Quality Meats. We made three more stops before all the errands were finished. We were leaving the Lathrop Building when Carl thought he recognized an old friend.

"Hey, Buck!" Carl yelled, stepping onto Second Avenue. "That you?" To me, Carl said, "From the back, that man looks just like Buck Rosenbush. Same black, knit ski cap pulled over his ears. Hair's whiter, but I'd know those long legs anywhere. Hey, Buck!"

The tall man loped on down the street and Carl quickened his pace. "Buck!"

The man turned. "Why, Carl Wilson!" he said, and shook Carl's hand forever.

They exchanged stories of the years since they last met. With another Alaskan by the name of Lyman, Buck Rosenbush once owned the Steel Creek roadhouse in the Forty Mile area. Carl met Buck several times through the years after Buck sold the roadhouse to Uncle Woody. Woody still owned the roadhouse but now he and Ruth lived in Wyoming.

"I heard you'd gone into the Hot Springs," Buck said. "Any possibility of me doing a little trapping up there this winter?"

"That country up Spring Creek hasn't been touched in years. Should be good." Carl said. "There's a few who trap below the Springs. I could give you work for room and board if you're interest-ed—some logging work, repair work. I plan on putting a roof on the swimming pool and replacing some logs in the old bathhouse. I have two other men lined up but I could use another person. You could do some trapping."

"That's right up my alley!" Buck said as he shook Carl's hand again and said he would be up when he got things in order. Chuck flew Carl back to the Springs.

By Friday Mom and I had finished packing up the house on Eighth Avenue and cleaned it up for the Strouds. Suzanne Stroud and her sister Joanne were school friends of mine. Suzanne belonged to the same Girl Scout troop I did. When I realized Suzanne was going to sleep in my room, I told her from now on I was going to school at the Springs. I even told her we were going to have our own teacher.

Mom arranged to put the bulk of our belongings in storage and Ann Bachner drove us to Hawley Evans' Fairbanks Air Service at Phillips Field. I sat in the co-pilot's seat beside him, the preferred position, while Mom took the back position in the rear of the twin Cessna, jammed in between boxes, supplies and suitcases, clutching Tweety Bird's cage on her lap. We'd had him since the days of Palmer, but he had spent the summer with Uncle Lyle and Aunt Pat in Fairbanks. Tweety Bird was searching a way out of his cage, flying to the top of the cage, clinging to the cage wires, flinging feathers everywhere.

I could hardly see over the instrument panel. I held my breath as Hawley banked against the hill and eased the plane toward the runway. Carl said Hawley was a pilot in World War II. In 1951, the year Denali School opened, Hawley, Joanne's dad, Jess Bachner, Dave Phillips and two other men from Fairbanks built Phillips Field where Chuck also kept his two planes. Hawley had owned Fairbanks Air Service for many years.

Hawley made a rough landing at the Springs. After he bounced the plane all the way to the end of the field, I made up my mind that from then on I would refuse to fly in Hawley's plane even if he asked me. I was worried about Tweety Bird, who seemed nervous about spending the winter at the Springs. He squawked all the way to the kitchen.

We found Smitty leaning against the sink, chewing on a cigar.

Carl and his crew built a cover over the open swimming pool during the first winter we were at the Springs, using three-sided logs after he got the old sawmill working and found good timber not too far away.

Mom's eyes surveyed the room. Pans of blueberries sat everywhere. Pots were scattered across the floor, filled with hard greasy stuff, and jars of jam lined one entire counter. Dirty dishes filled the kitchen sink, stacked higher than the windowsill. I pointed to a large steel pot underneath the long counter filled with more of the slick muck. "What's in there?" I asked.

"Lye soap," Smitty said past a cigar and the gaps where teeth should have been. "Couldn't get those boys of yours to eat a thing—said they were going to wait for you to get home." His sweaty white hair stuck out beneath the rim of the finger-smudged chef's hat that drooped over his eyes. He needed a shave.

Mom looked at Carl. Carl looked at Smitty.

Three big boxes from Baltimore arrived with the next mail drop. There was also a letter from the army: two groups of men were hiking to Chena Hot Springs. The first group was due in a couple of days, so we weren't to open the box from the Calvert School until later. Mom was very firm.

"By the time the second bunch of soldiers gets here, we'll have corned caribou," Smitty announced. "I'll make veal cutlets. I can soak caribou in that old crock behind the laundry room door. They'll never know what they are eating." He said Walt had to rearrange his schedule because the Model Café wanted him to cook at the same time the second group was to arrive. Smitty said he would help cook for the second group until Walt came back for him.

A caribou hunt was planned to the Rock House, one of our favorite hunting spots nearby. The next morning Smitty and I cleaned the blueberries he and the boys had picked while we had been in town.

"Let the wind do the work," Smitty said. "Pour from pan to pan outdoors."

Smitty made bread in washtubs and dishpans and kettles. He made blueberry spiced jam, and cherry syrup with the juice he saved from the canned cherries he used for pies. I stuck blueberries in dinner rolls and sweet breads and muffins and was told never to say the word *caribou*.

Smitty reviewed his mental list aloud. "We can cook up some stew, curry, soup, casserole, and make sandwiches with leftover turkey, fried chicken, roast beef and ham."

It was a 50-mile walk for the men. One by one the first group of green tents puffed up across the hillside above Spring Creek. Some of the men camped above the airfield. I lay in bed smiling as their laughter erupted every few minutes, drifting over the gurgling creek. Their lanterns twinkled against the hillside like stars in the sky.

Blisters kept most of the men in the bathhouse soaking their sore feet the next day. The few who were able climbed the "Big Hill" after breakfast. On payday, the men played cards in the Lodge and Carl tended bar till after three in the morning.

Over the course of the week, Mom, Smitty and I prepared three family-style settings each day for evening meals. Boy, could those men eat. Lunch was available for those who wanted it. We worked long and hard preparing potato, macaroni and Jell-O salads, vegetable dishes, meats, corn bread, muffins, and fresh baked bread.

By the time the second group of soldiers arrived, the morning sun lacked the heat of summer. Carl, Red, and Jim had been working daily at the old sawmill to get it in running order before Buck arrived.

I served apple, cherry, blueberry, mince, lemon, or pumpkin pies to soldiers who didn't look much older than Rocky and Terry, but were already so disciplined. I could imagine them bravely defending our country against the Russians. A few soldiers were really cute, but I didn't mention it to anyone because Carl had given me one of those little talking-to sessions before the first group of men arrived.

"Soldiers all look the same in uniform, Gwen. You don't know what they are really like until they are out of uniform. And then they may turn out to be what you had never imagined," Carl said in a serious tone. I nodded slowly.

When the last of Col. Greer's troops lumbered down the winter trail, leafless, skinny tree branches pointed to an armored gray October sky. I watched the men set out on their long hike back to Eielson AFB, their cadenced footsteps echoing long after they were out of sight. I could still hear their rhythmic gait as they continued on past Sully's sod-roofed cabin at the North Fork. A few of the boys faces flashed in my mind for a moment; I wondered what it would have been like if I had had a chance to get to know them, even if they were in uniform.

Smitty was right. They never knew if they had eaten veal cutlets or caribou.

CHAPTER 18

Winter of 1909

The Register and Receiver of the Fairbanks land office wrote a letter on February 9, 1909, to the Commissioner of the General Land Office in Washington D.C., addressing George Wilson's concern that the government might withdraw the land he had filed on from public entry because it was a valuable mineral springs.

Commissioner S.V. Proudfit in Washington replied to the letter, stating his office did not fully understand by what authority George Wilson was informed he could not get title to the land under the homestead laws. Proudfit did not think there was a good reason to refuse George's filing merely because the Fairbanks office anticipated that the land might later be the subject of government reservation. Unless the government had already set aside the land because it contained sulphur springs with potential medicinal use, to which the Fairbanks office had referred, Commissioner Proudfit saw no reason why George couldn't claim the land as a homestead. George replied.

April 15, 1909

To the General Land Office
Washington, D.C.:
As a Homestead(er) I have filed on 160 acres of land in Fairbanks district and have made a good lot of improvement in the way of buildings and clearing the land for cultivation. On the said Homestead

there is a hot springs and I have been told the Government may see fit some day to reserve the same. Then offer leases.

Were the Government to take such action, Can I secure the lease. And how?

I was entitled to 320 acres of land at the time I staked it but not being familiar with the homestead law at the time, I only staked 160 acres. Can I secure the other half if the same is unoccupied or has not yet been staked by anyone else.

Please send me instructions and a copy of Homestead and timber laws of Alaska. This would be information seen by many people and I should like to have the same in a fact, or a form, that I could post it on a tree or where it would be seen by the many curious people who have visited my homestead.

Also, a copy of the timber laws as I wish to protect the same from fire set by campers. As stick fires drive the game out of the country and destroys timber for miles.

Hoping to hear from you soon, I remain yours truly,
George W. Wilson
Chena Hot Springs
Fairbanks Dist. Alaska

George's new bathhouse was large, 16 feet by 36 feet, built over one of the hot springs, fed by a box line tapping a hot spring located about 100 feet above the building and by a spring directly under the bathhouse. He planned to divide the bathhouse into three areas: a dressing room, a sweat room directly over an area of hot ground, and a third room with tubs for a water bath and a mud bath. With break-up expected soon, George knew it would be awhile before he could get to town. When he did make the trip to Fairbanks for supplies he rented a room at the Northern Hotel. He hoped there would be a letter waiting for him, but there was not.

As the winter snows began to melt, George Wilson, Charley Boyer and Floyd Blankenship prepared a one-quarter acre of ground for cultivation. The cost of clearing was estimated at $300 an acre.

The section they worked included the small garden area George had cleared when he staked the homestead. They dug out the stumps from the trees felled for George's log cabin the previous fall.

Mrs. Beam leases the Hot Springs property from George Wilson for five years and the couple entertain a fair number of guests. Shown here is Charley Beam on the left and Mrs. Beam on the extreme right. On the horse is a lady with mosquito net and a child. *(Courtesy National Archives.)*

On May 2, 1909, the ice broke in Fairbanks. With long, thick ropes and a donkey engine, men scurried to tow the center section of the Cushman Street Bridge to safety before the ice smashed it into kindling. Residents gathered along the riverfront to watch. When the ice did go, whistles blew, church bells rang and when the ice jammed, dynamite blasted it apart in an attempt to prevent a flood. It seemed the whole town had turned out for the excitement.

The bridge was pulled to safety but another devastating flood hit Fairbanks. For three weeks the river carried enormous amounts of run-off waters to the Tanana River.

Finally, an answer came to George's letter. The government's response was dated June 3, 1909. "If you have initiated a valid claim to the land upon which such a spring is located, it is hardly probable that it will be reserved for any purpose in any way which would defeat your right." The letter was signed "Fred Dennett, Commissioner."

In July, Charley Boyer's old partner heard Charley was going to loan George money. He told Charley to ask George, in an off-hand way, if George was a citizen of the United States. "If George wasn't a citizen, maybe some of those other gentlemen at the Hot Springs could stake the homestead for themselves. Boyer would have to get off as well as George," his friend told him. Charley thought it a good idea, so he asked.

In answer to Boyer's question, George stated that it was only necessary to show full citizenship at the date of proving up. He was living in Michigan when he turned twenty-one. Charley Slater, then living in Fairbanks, could vouch for him. George said he could take out final naturalization papers any time without a formal preliminary declaration because his status was similar to one who had already declared his intention.

George, concerned that his foreign citizenship might impact his homesteading claim, decided it was time to get the matter cleared up. At 35 minutes past 10 A.M. on July 25, 1909, George signed an amended homestead location notice at the courthouse in Fairbanks, to correct errors in the original location and to verify that all necessary paperwork was in order. The next day, George declared his intention to become a citizen of the United States.

His amended location notice for 320 acres instead of 160 acres was recorded July 27, 1909, showing the southeast corner stake about 20 feet south of Spring Creek and about one-quarter mile above the confluence of the creek with Monument Creek, one mile long from east to west, and one-half mile wide from north to south.

Charley Boyer loaned George the hundred dollars.

෴

While George and Charley were digging stumps later that summer they welcomed an unexpected guest. Lewis T. Erwin, then a private citizen, came riding onto George's homestead on a breachy mule. While there, the mule broke into George's garden more than once, causing frequent clashes between Erwin and George.

In 1904, Lewis T. Erwin left Dawson where he found some success mining, hoping Fairbanks would have more to offer. Soon after his arrival, he was elected city magistrate, and served for two years. Some residents found the "Judge," as he was called, arrogant, with an air of morally superiority, speaking in a magnolia-draped Georgian accent. His breath frequently smelled of late night mint juleps. Others said he beat his wife, yet still, the town viewed him as a solid investment. George heard that L.T. Erwin would "fix" him on the homestead matter.

Before the river froze that fall, George filed a second amended homestead location notice on September 23, 1909. He described a tract one mile long from north to south and one-half mile wide from east to west. All three locations covered the land where the Hot Springs were located.

The Lease of 1911

In early 1911 the trail to Big Chena Hot Springs was packed solid with snow, on the heels of an unusually bitter winter. Temperatures had reached minus 50 degrees and lower in many of the mining camps and settlements surrounding Fairbanks. Work in the mine shafts ground to a halt. Steam heat in the shafts was being kept at minimums, just above the freezing point, to conserve wood supplies.

It was a time for miners to take advantage of the break from the grueling mine work. They washed their heavy work clothes with hot water from the boiler houses, played cards and caught up on much-needed rest. Others took a jaunt to the Hot Springs to soak their aching bodies.

Traffic from Fairbanks in February was heavy. Miners, prospectors, health-seekers and residents of Fairbanks left work, the comfort of their heated homes and their daily routines behind for a relaxing vacation at the Big Chena Hot Springs. Old friends reunited and new friends got acquainted, as the resort guests compared the struggles of life in the coldest land they had ever known.

As the Springs grew in popularity as a winter destination, locals pressed the territorial government for a road from Fairbanks. In 1913 the Alaska Road Commission obliged, and built a winter trail to the Springs. Four roadhouses were now either open or nearly finished, complete with stables, catering to the new traffic. Colorado Creek was the largest roadhouse, about halfway along the three or four-day dogsled route from Fairbanks.

George's new bathhouse had three rooms: first, the dressing room, then the sweat room, with about a dozen slabs so guests could lie down and soak up the heat from the earth, since George had built the structure over the hottest ground on the property. From the sweat room they entered the third room, the bath-room, which contained five bathtubs and a mud bath.

Together, friends and guests soaked away their worries and disappointments, relaxed by sharing the warm water and conversation. At least for a little while, the bathers paid no attention to the severe cold and wind that waited on the other side of the spruce logs of George's brand new bathhouse.

On March 28, 1911 (in accordance with the act of June 25th, 1910) President Taft withdrew from settlement, location, sale, or entry, "all tracts of public lands in the District of Alaska, upon which [exist] hot springs, or other springs, the waters of which possess curative medicinal properties." This move to protect public lands from private interest followed naturally from Roosevelt's earlier Square Deal program. FDR's friend Gifford Pinchot pioneered the first national conservation initiative for stewarding natural resources like farms, forests, hot springs and range lands. It is not know when news of Taft's executive order reached George Wilson.

George continued to allow the public onto his land. When the weather turned warm and the ice broke in the rivers, George hired Tom Roberts to freight supplies by boat from Fairbanks. On one of Tom's May trips upriver to the Springs, he arrived with passengers, Mr. & Mrs. Charles Beam, John Connors and Jack Lindsay. The Beams were a good-natured couple, known for their honest dealings, who had lived in Fairbanks about six years before they first visited the Springs in 1908. Now they returned to make use of the healing pools again. The Beams paid George fifty cents per bath, trying out the new bathhouse located about 100 feet from the Springs.

On this visit, the Beams took more than casual interest in the Springs. Charles Beam observed that the water in the bath house was "about 130 (degrees) or 135 in the bath tubs as it comes into the tubs. There are different springs at different heat; some of them are lower than that."

Dr. LeBlanc, a physician based in Fairbanks, had been eager to analyze the water at the Hot Springs. He asked Tom Roberts to collect a sample for him to have tested.

"I told him to bring me a gallon of it," LeBlanc said later in a statement. Charley Beam went ahead and filled a few beer bottles—"the only way he had to bring it in." LeBlanc in turn sent the samples to Judge Wickersham who took the "tightly sealed glass receptacles" to the Department of Agriculture in Washington, D.C. At first the agency refused to accept or analyze the water because it had not been drawn by a government official, but Wickersham would not be deterred. Eventually the Bureau of Chemistry "concluded that the water was 'different from any American hot springs which we have examined.'" The Chena Hot Springs water contained (among other components) sulphate, chloride and bicarbonate of sodium. Though in lower concentrations, the percentage composition of the mineral salts was most similar to that of the Felsenquelle, a famous thermal springs at Carlsbad, Bohemia.

The analysis confirmed what others had learned by experience—this particular mineral springs offered health benefits that visitors would travel long distances to try for themselves. On July 7th in Fairbanks, a lease was drawn up between George Wilson and I. M. Beam, wife of Charley Beam, for "that certain health resort known as the Chena River Hot Springs, consisting of twelve cabins used as residences, with a stable and bath house, with the use of the mineral waters necessary to carry on such health resort, and the use of sufficient land for such purposes." It was a five-year lease, the first year costing $1200 and then $1500 for each of the remaining four years. "We intended to run a health resort," Mrs. Beam said. "We took it with that idea."

"We didn't get there until about the 7th, I believe," Charles Beam said. "We were delayed on the river. We were supposed to have possession the 1st of August, 1911. I think we were about 12 days going up. We were loaded pretty heavily." The laborious river route still involved poling boats.

"George had about seven and one-half to ten acres cleared. He had most of this sowed to oats. His main crop was oat, (then) hay, spuds, and vegetables. The oats ran about two tons to the acre and the spuds were a good crop," said Charles Beam.

There were quite a number of tents there besides the cabins. The Beams charged $20 a month for the cabins, some for $15 and $10. They charged $12.50 a month for the tents. They also kept boarders who stayed in the hotel building on the land and charged $15.00 a month for baths. The revenue from boarders helped cover the resort's basic operating costs.

In those years, Charles advertised Chena Hot Springs as the "Most Famous Health Resort" of Interior Alaska, and it very well may have been. The Beams ran a modest but steady business. Not only did the waters cure many physical ailments, but the Beams were enthusiastic hosts. Visitors praised them for serving fabulous meals, reinvesting their profits to improve the facilities, and in general, "doing all in their power to make the stay of the health-seekers pleasant."

As much as townspeople took to the Beams, they seemed to disagree with George Wilson on many counts. In September 1911, around the time George got married in Fairbanks, some angry townsfolk filed charges against Mr. Wilson, to be investigated by the Grand Jury. The plaintiffs charged George with the "malicious destruction of certain cabins and other property on the land he had homesteaded." First, Wilson had leveled the "private" cabins that a few visitors built on the land for public use, after the Swans' discovery but before Wilson laid claim to the area as a homestead. Second, Wilson had torn down the cabins McCauley, Douse and Heacock built during their November 1908 visit, including the original Swan brothers' cabin they had enlarged. Despite numerous testimonies by the prosecution, the Commissioner's Court exonerated George.

While the legal battles continued in Fairbanks, business at the Springs continued unabated. Louis Behl, working the Bonnifield country, was in route to work on his claim on Bedrock Bar on the Middle Fork of the Big Chena River. On his way through he stopped in at the Hot Springs. "Because the trail goes up by there. You can't go no other way," Behl said. "I stopped there one night...at Charley Beam's in a cabin."

"Why, when I was taking the bath...in Mr. Wilson's bath house... he came in, and he was taking a bath, and he wanted me to pay for the rent of that bath house—hold on, now. He wanted me to pay for the groceries I owed him, that is it," Behl said, "for the time I was there in 1910."

"He said, 'You owe me seven dollars for the groceries. I says I don't. I says if I owe you anything, I owe you for the bath house and the rent of the tent. He said it aint worth fighting for. He said it was not worthwhile. And he left."

By now, several roadhouses were established between Fairbanks and the Hot Springs. Stage trips were scheduled from Fairbanks over the winter trail regularly and passengers were able to stop for overnight lodging and meals at the convenient roadside locations.

John Mihalcik, a miner at Ready Bullion, and living in the Fairbanks area for about eight years, had suffered from rheumatism since August to the point where he could no longer walk. On November 16 he hired a private rig, a double-ender (sled) and arrived at the Hot Springs four days later.

"The doctor told me it was sciatic rheumatism," Mihalcik said.

Mihalcik, an Austrian and naturalized citizen of the United States, suffered greatly. When he arrived at Fairbanks he could hardly walk the streets. The rheumatism was so severe in his back and left leg that he was frequently bedridden. His friends in Fairbanks had urged Mihalcik to try the curing waters of the Big Chena Hot Springs east of Fairbanks.

"I took about two baths a day," Mihalcik said. "Sometimes I would lay off a day and take one. I took about eighty-five baths and drank the water every day."

J. H. Groves, a resident of Fairbanks, had taken his own horse and double-ender over the trail. "Well, I had rheumatism in one knee pretty bad and couldn't get rid of it," said Groves, "and went up there to see the Springs. I saw a great many there during the time I was there...so many that I scarcely remember the names of more than one or two, Mihalcik and a lady. There was (sic) perhaps eight or nine men there at the time."

Before every meal, Mihalcik made his way from the cabin he had rented to the pool and drank the hot water. After thirty days, he began to feel better. He continued to improve. On January 10, 1912, he returned to town.

Shortly after Mihalcik left, George made a trip to town for supplies. He arrived in Fairbanks on Thursday, the 18th of January. The next day, the *Fairbanks Daily News-Miner* ran this headline: "Patients in Good Health: Mr. Wilson reports that the parties at the Springs who now number 25, are all well and in good spirits. Several of them will return to Fairbanks on the next trip of the Dilley State, which should arrive Monday or Tuesday." (*Fairbanks Daily News-Miner*, January 19, 1912)

The article described the roadhouse accommodations between Fairbanks and the Hot Springs as "good." The paper went on to say, "In fact, they are a greatly appreciated boon to those who had to provide their own accommodations a few years ago, when the trip to the springs was made." The article said the trail to the Hot Springs was reportedly in the best condition that it had ever been. Jack Connor, a well-known physical culturist, had recently opened a roadhouse between Little Chena and Colorado Creek.

When John Mihalcik returned to Fairbanks in early January walking upright, agent John Barker paid him a visit. Two months earlier, in November 1911, the Field Division of the Federal Land Office had directed Special Agent John W. Barker to make an on-site inspection of George Wilson's homestead. He had already begun his thorough investigation.

The demolition of cabins built by McCauley and the others during the winter of 1908 was first called to the attention of District Attorney James J. Crossley when several Fairbanksans complained that justice had not been served. At that time, George had been tried and acquitted in the Commissioner's Court at Fairbanks. But the plaintiffs were not satisfied, now arguing to the Land Office that since President Taft protected natural resources like forests and medicinal springs from private, commercial use, George had no right to the Springs. American-born citizens were abiding by the new law. So should *the Canadian*, as they called him.

On February 11th, Agent Barker arrived at George Wilson's homestead armed with a Kodak camera. Barker found 14 cabins, six tents, a bathhouse and a barn. Twelve cabins were used to rent to patrons, as were the tents. The Beams used another cabin facing the creek as a bunkhouse and storeroom.

Barker reported 12 acres had been partially cleared by cutting down the trees where all the buildings were situated. Immediately surrounding them, an irregular tract of about five acres had been cleared of everything. Wilson had raised a few potatoes and vegetables for table use and to sell to those visiting the Springs. He said the snow on the ground prevented an accurate measurement, but not over two acres had been placed under that sort of cultivation. Barker said the buildings surrounding the Springs had the appearance of a small village, novel in its seclusion, and at this season, of unspoiled beauty.

"The scene is impressive, breaking suddenly out of the forest into this clearing after two and one-half days' travel through a stretch of country populated only by four roadhouse keepers who make their living feeding people passing between Fairbanks and this resort," Barker wrote.

The steam, or vapor, Barker reported, rises at times in such density as to almost obscure the buildings beyond, the sulfurous odor permeating the air noticeably to newcomers. He found the water had a temperature of 158 degrees and was conducted to the bathhouse by means of a crude pipeline. To complete his report, Barker inspected the bathhouse, the five tubs in the bathing room, the steam room and the sweat room.

In February 1912, Barker reported that in his assessment, Mr. Wilson's stake was invalid. Wilson's "agricultural purposes" cited in his original homestead claim amounted to no more than "any fisherman along the rivers, or any roadhouse keeper, would do in this country for his own table." Barker opined that Wilson was more interested in the Springs for their profit potential, so Wilson's claim to the land as a homestead was invalid, violating the spirit of the Homestead Act. He recommended that the Wilson patent be denied. Even if George had legitimately farmed the land, the waters of Chena Hot Springs were generally considered to have "a curative quality second to none in the United States," so Barker objected to private ownership on conservationist principles. In his view, a natural resources so beneficial to the public should be accessible, not privatized.

1913-1916 saw more legal wrangling, first denying Wilson's claim. Upon appeal, the Department of the Interior overturned the lower court's decision and considered Wilson's homestead claim valid. George was finally naturalized as a U.S. citizen in 1918 and received his patent for homestead the following year, eleven years after originally staking his claim.

George got married in Fairbanks in September of 1911. He and his wife raised a small family on the Hot Springs property at least until 1916. After an exhaustive search of public records, no further details have surfaced about George's later life and death.

CHAPTER 19

The First Year

The Fort

The weekend before I turned thirteen the boys asked me if I wanted to help build a fort in the woods below the Rock Towers, near Spring Creek. We hiked to the old sawmill beside Spring Creek where Terry and Rocky proceeded to cut down long willows.

"Dig deep holes and stand the willows in the holes," Rocky directed.

The boys were using pocket knives Carl had given them for Christmas. Prior to the walk to the fort site I searched the shelf above the forge in George's stable, and found a large, cleaver-type knife with a wooden handle. I was almost certain the knife was from the olden days, touched by Indians and probably from a trade with the Russians in exchange for pretty colored beads, or bowls and spoons. How George got it I couldn't imagine but he had to have used it. He would have needed a knife like that when he boated the supplies up from Fairbanks and built the stable. Most likely he was the one who had put the knife on the shelf. To me, it was very special.

Now I carved deep holes into the dirt with it and I was getting tired of digging but I considered the fort project one of great importance because it was the only time Rocky and Terry ever let me be a part of anything they had in mind to do as grand as this.

The remains of an old log bear trap near the mill had prompted the fort idea. Built on the other side of Spring Creek across from the old sawmill and against the side hill, the bear trap had been built of round logs, three times the size of an ordinary dog house. Lured by bait placed inside the log trap, the bear would enter, tripping a trap door that kept him inside until the trapper came and shot him. I wanted to think George built the structure for storing food, but Carl said it wasn't true.

The Wilson kids enjoyed family excursions on the Weasel to various places in the Hot Springs area. The anticipation shows on their faces as they and Totem embark on a trip to the Maclaren River in Southcentral Alaska.

Soon the skinny willows were standing upright in the holes I'd dug, looking like walls. We then proceeded to weave reeds in the standing willows like a basket. The walls were a little floppy.

"Boy, wait until Mom and Carl see this," said Rocky.

When Carl moved the sawmill, it had wrecked the boys' special hideaway. The original sawmill had been built next to Spring Creek, near the Lodge. Some time later it was moved further down the creek near the base of the hill where the creek made a bend around the hill beneath the Rock Towers.

I plunged the knife into the dirt to dig another hole. But as I did the knife slipped and l fell forward. As I attempted to regain my balance the rusty knife blade cut between my thumb and index finger.

Blood spurted everywhere.

Carl and the boys and occasionally others help log in the North Fork area. The area provided building material for as many as 30 recreational cabins for Fairbanks residents. The old sawmill, located near the log truck, was somewhat portable.

Terry screamed and ran for the Lodge. Rocky said, "Now you've done it. I knew we shouldn't let you help. Mom and Carl won't let us do it now. You've ruined everything."

Mom made me soak my hand in a dishpan full of Epsom salts and warm water. Later, on the verge of tears, my hand turned a horrible purple.

"My hand is going to fall off. It's dead," I said. A rusty orange and red scab, now covered only part of the wound, and it was getting mushy and turning an ugly gold color. "My skin is rotting!" I said.

"Your skin is not rotting," Mom assured me. "It's beginning to heal."

"It doesn't look healed to me." I raised my hand from the solution and took a closer look.

Cabin building provided an income in our early days at the Springs. Most of them were recreational cabins for people in Fairbanks. Carl obtained five-acre plots from the state and placed a finished cabin on the site for a given price. He built about 30 cabins in all.

"Keep your hand in the bath, Gwennie."

I soaked my hand three times a day until the swelling went down. The boys were not on speaking terms with me. The fort in the woods was off limits to them and I was back to being the sheriff in search of outlaws, chasing Rocky and Terry through the woods and locking them up in the meat shack.

∽

Calvert Schooling

That first year we didn't finish school by the first of April like we thought we would. We did, however, beat the town kids getting out of school. We finished before my birthday in May.

When we went to the Springs I was 12 years old, Rocky 10, and Terry nine years old. I only had two years of school at the Springs— 7th and 8th grade Calvert Courses—until I went to town for high school. What I do remember is the Calvert Course was exceptionally thorough, conducted at home without interruptions.

Mom sent our homework, assignments and tests to our teachers in Baltimore. The teachers would correct them and send us grades and wish us well in our "nontraditional" education.

> *Calvert School*
> *Home Instruction Department*
> *My Dear Gwen,*
>
> *It was unfortunate that you have injured your hand and had so much difficulty in writing; however, the injury has not prevented you from doing praiseworthy work on test 160. I think that you can be very proud of these tests, Gwen, and I am very proud of you.*
>
> *Although school is over, please check the corrections on these tests and master the facts. Be certain that you understand the corrections in grammar and arithmetic for they are important.*
>
> *You have been a very ambitious pupil and you have completed this Course most successfully. Your record is one of which you can be*

proud, Gwen. It makes me very happy to award the Certificate for the completion of the seventh grade Course.

    I hope that you will have a pleasant vacation. For now you can relax and know that your work was well done.
Affectionately yours,
Mildred J. Phillips

That same spring Carl decided we should have some Sunday School lessons. A box came with the mail several weeks later from the Presbyterian church in Fairbanks. Lessons didn't last very long because the boys didn't like that I was their teacher. The box was full of all kinds of books and games and puzzles. When we lived in town and were much younger Mom always carted us down Eighth Avenue in the little red wagon to First Presbyterian Church on Cushman Street for Sunday School. Carl always said that because we didn't have a church, we could go out under a tree and talk to God there. In fact, he said we should because God made every tree.

❧

Birthday at the Springs

Chena Hot Springs, Alaska
May 3, 1955
Dear Gwen:
We didn't get a chance to go to town to get you a gift.
So we give you money to buy one when you can and
   what you want.
   HAPPY BIRTHDAY
   Carl, Belle, Rocky and Terry

Aunt Pat along with Uncle Lyle Wilson visited during one of our first years at the Springs. Belle on the left, Gwen fixing her hair for the picture, and Pat.

❧

Family Dog Mushing

Carl eventually cut a trail all the way up Monument Creek to the base of Far Mountain, then later on to Clums Fork of Birch Creek. He built a small cabin of three-sided logs at the base of the mountain which he called a recreation cabin for the family.

Carl was very proud of his Mackenzie River dog team, adapted to deep snow conditions and cold weather. All were a similar tan color, named, from left, Sugar, Bones, Chamie, Dipper, Pat, Mike, and Frosty the leader.

Carl put together a team of large sled dogs. He got the first pups, Tina and Piper, from Les and Millie Jacobson. He later went to northern Canada with a friend and purchased some Mackenzie River sled pups, a very large, strong breed used in deep snow conditions. He also got some dogs from Gus Lohai, who lived a lonely life near where Munson Creek runs into the Middle Fork. Our lead dog, Frosty, was half wolf and very smart. Totem moved more slowly these days, and seemed to enjoy having some company that spoke her language.

Before long, Carl had a good team of large, tough dogs. We used the dogsled for trapping up the creeks, and for winter transportation in general, since the road to the Hot Springs was still in its planning stages. Friends living near town let us keep our dogsled hitched at their house so we could come the rest of the way from Fairbanks to the Springs by sled.

Dipper was a littermate of one of our swing dogs (first in front of the dogsled). He had a floppy ear which was, for awhile, held up with masking tape until it would finally stay upright.

About this time the Dog Mushers' Association in Fairbanks contacted Carl about their members making an expedition to the Springs in March. Carl encouraged this; they came, camped, used our facilities and had a good time. They repeated this for several years.

210

They were even joined by some of the early snow-machiners from town. Years later, even when Carl's health was failing, he wanted to keep some large dogs for the tourists to see and photograph.

The dogs were well-kept with good houses and cooked food, dried salmon, grain, and sometimes, table scraps. Carl took a lot of pride in breeding and caring for the dogs. Often one or two were brought into the Lodge. All were tame and safe among visitors.

A Future Road to the Springs

For years, local leaders had talked about building a road from Fairbanks to open the Upper Chena Valley and terminate at the Springs or even continue over to Birch Creek and connect with the Steese Highway at Central, offering an alternate route to the Upper Yukon Valley. My folks welcomed the improved access, as a way to increase exposure to the resort.

Crews showed up for preliminary surveying in 1955, eating meals at the Lodge and going for swims in the evening. Additional crews were surveying other homestead land near the North Fork. Walt Belling, cook at the Model Café in town, was dividing parts of his land into lots for future development.

A short while after noon on a Sunday, George Silides and his crew of surveyors flew in. We had hosted a large group of people for dinner the night before, so Mom and I made a mad dash to the dining room to clear away the dishes from the tables before the men walked through the front door of the Lodge.

In my haste to the kitchen, I flung the cake I was carrying into the wood box. I knew George was right behind me. Embarrassed, I ducked behind the island table and frantically tried on my hands and knees to clean up the mess, as George walked into the kitchen.

Mom was standing by the stove. She flashed me a disapproving expression. The next moment she turned toward George, with a gracious "Hello." I knew if George hadn't been in the kitchen she would have said, "Gwendolyn! For Pete's sake, why don't you watch what you're doing?"

I figured Mr. Silides could actually see me there behind the table, so I didn't know whether to stand up or stay down, hiding. After a few moments I raised my head, my nose even with the top of the table, just to where I could see him, and squeaked, "Hi!" Gladly, he chuckled, and later we laughed as we cleaned up the mess. Our family worked hard, but had no problem laughing when a situation was obviously silly.

It would be another decade before a road was actually constructed, but eventually a gravel road connected the Springs with Fairbanks, after I had left for school in town.

Caribou Ranch

Joanne Bachner was coming to visit for two weeks in July. Carl had told us that at the end of her visit we could make the trip to Caribou Ranch. Carl planned to take the M29 Weasel he recently bought from town, a surplus WWII army vehicle that the first Special Services used to travel quickly over the heavy snows of Norway. I looked forward to this trip for several days. In the meantime, Mom and Carl gave the order that if we had guests, Joanne and I would wait tables together.

The first week raced by. Joanne and I played Monopoly, went swimming, and walked to Monument Creek without the boys, to do some fishing. On Friday I washed Joanne's hair and gave her a new "do." She hated it so much she washed it out before we went downstairs to work.

On Tuesday of the next week, following a big weekend of guests for meals and swims, we packed up the Weasel for the Caribou Ranch. We left the North Fork and crawled along low, mossy hillsides and small green valleys before we entered a rocky canyon hidden within the hills.

"Caribou country," Carl said, slowing the Weasel down. "That's how this place got here in the first place. The people who used to live here wanted to raise caribou like beef, sell the meat. And they did for awhile, I've been told."

In the late teens or early 1920s a family attempted an almost impossible feat further up the North Fork. They built a two-story log house in a secluded valley about five miles above the Springs. They transported large rolls of six-foot-high fencing, like heavyweight chicken wire, to the location. They intended to fence in enough of the area to catch and retain caribou.

The house at the end of the canyon seemed to float in the air; the log siding glistened in the afternoon sun above the willows that crowded the narrow valley. From a distance, the house appeared occupied. But the closer we got, the more the abandoned house looked haunted, neglect having destroyed a once-bustling family home. The small trail leading through the canyon was barely visible.

The log house had been built on a rise of ground that looked across a large basin of wilderness. The walls sagged. The roof was still trying to hold its own, but I knew it would never make it. Carl stopped the Weasel. Near the front entrance the remains of a small garden angled around to the back of the house.

The caribou roamed those lands in great herds. Passing through this secluded basin, they entered tunnels of fencing and were corralled to graze and bear their young. Where animals had been contained, you could still make out small, overgrown meadows. There were rolls of fencing that were never used to completely enclose the basin.

The owners were unsuccessful in their attempt to run a profitable business off God's creatures within these secluded hills, so they had left many years before. Not unlike most deserted sites in the wilderness, they had also left behind many of their belongings.

The inside of the home had been thoroughly searched by wild animals. "Bears," Carl said, "or wolverine." It made me sad, to think of the excitement they must have felt when they carted in all their stuff over the winter trail, past the Springs. All their furniture and dishes and everything, now a heap of rubble.

There was a fine oak buffet, broken plates and bowls, beautiful tall glass oil lamps, stacks of *National Geographic* magazines dating from the early 1900s. On the floor under some old clothes I found a large, pink seashell from a far-off ocean. I turned it over and inside, were shiny silver specks.

I tucked the shell into my backpack, thinking whoever had left it sure liked nice things. Why would they leave everything after taking so much trouble to get it all in here? I decided I would not ask. We camped overnight in that deserted place, which felt kind of eerie.

Chuck told us later that he had met a daughter from the family that lived there. Around 1955 Milt Reed installed a hot air furnace in Chuck's home in town. At that time, Milt mentioned to Chuck that his wife, the shop bookkeeper, was raised at the Caribou Ranch. Chuck stopped in at Reed's Sheet Metal shop later to pay his bill and talked briefly to Mrs. Reed. Not having been to the Caribou Ranch himself, he didn't know enough about the location to ask the questions I wanted answered. At that time Mrs. Reed appeared to be about 50 years old.

When we got back from the Caribou Ranch, Joanne and I continued working on the three one-act plays. Early Friday night directly after supper we arranged chairs in the Lodge and presented the plays for my family and the resort guests.

$\sim$

Grandparents' Visit

In the summer of 1955, Grandpa and Grandma Heller came from Seattle to visit for a month. They seemed to enjoy the rhythms of everyday life at our rustic resort. Chuck met their flight from Seattle at the Fairbanks airport and flew them up to the Springs in his Cessna. Frosty, Tina and Piper became Grandma's little pets. She also liked my pet squirrel that ran for hours on its exercise wheel. (I let him go free when he got too big for his cage.) The weather remained in the mid-sixties. Grandpa fished a lot down at the North Fork. He decked himself out in fishing gear and spent many hours getting ready. Grandpa also took photos of our "pet" fox, Raynard, that Mom fed kitchen scraps out of her hand. I loved all of our unusual animals.

Every Friday afternoon, while visiting with Grandma in the guest room, I painted my fingernails with nail polish. She told me stories of Mom as a little girl, growing up in Juneau and Haines, and of little Bobby, the boy they took in as one of their family. I would recognize later that a special bond developed between Grandma and me that August––one that continued to grow each summer when they came to visit again.

Christmas, Wilson-Style

As Christmas approached on our second winter at the Springs, Carl wanted us to have a real Christmas. He just had to open the old winter trail to town or bust! He spent over a week with the D4 Cat in the low December daylight clearing a path to meet the Steele Creek road east of Fairbanks. He got back to the Springs just four days before Christmas.

We all left the next day for town, stuffed in the old 6x6 truck. It took over 12 hours before we arrived late at night at the Bachners' home. The next day we split up at the Northern Commercial Co.

store to shop for each other. We also spent time at other stores and enjoyed the bright Christmas lights and decorations around town.

After a whirlwind trip to town for Christmas shopping and braving the elements to get back to the Springs, the family arrived the day after Christmas glad to open presents together.

That night it turned bitter cold—fifty below zero. Friends tried to convinced us to delay our return to the Springs, but Carl couldn't wait any longer to celebrate Christmas. We headed home for the Springs, stopping along the way to cut a nice white spruce tree, and we celebrated Christmas a day late. We all had a good laugh when we found that Mom and I had bought the same wool skirt for each other.

CHAPTER 20

Between Fairbanks and The Springs

Emergency Flight to Town

After supper one December night Rocky developed a bad pain in his lower stomach. As it gradually got worse my folks decided it would be best to get him to town in case the problem was his appendix.

Carl had a radio hookup with Wien Airlines in Fairbanks because we were on a mail drop served by Wien's and they needed weather reports on mail days. Carl called them to see if they could dispatch one of their bush planes to the Springs that night. They told us it would be impossible because as a commercial operator they were not authorized to fly at night into an unlighted airfield. Besides, it was snowing!

Then Carl asked them to call Chuck Gray to see if it would be safe for him to make the flight. The word came back that he would try it but he would have to warm the engine and prep his ski-equipped Cub. We all guessed it would take about three hours to get there if he could get through. And how could we light the runway for a landing?

Carl said we could put the jeep at one end of the runway, shining the lights on the snow. On the other end we made two flares using buckets with diesel-soaked rags. We would light them if we heard an airplane.

Chuck arrived just about when we thought he would. He flew up Monument Valley, turned and came down for a landing. He had made so many landings on our runway that I think he could do it with his eyes closed. Doing it in the snowstorm isn't that much different, I suppose.

"It wasn't too bad," Chuck said when he jumped out of the cockpit. "The snow was light all the way and I didn't run into any low scud."

Rocky, left and Terry, with two of their dogs, Red Dog on the left and Totem. After Totem died in 1960, the Wilsons never had another house dog.

Rocky was bundled up and a robe was put around him in the back seat of the Cub. Chuck said the flight back was uneventful. He told us later that when he got near town, the city lights looked pretty good to him! He landed back at his regular airfield, Phillips Field, and rushed Rocky to the old hospital on Garden Island. It was the next morning that the hospital reported it was not appendicitis—just a bad bellyache. The Wien radio operator was good enough to pass that good news on to us at the Springs.

Big Bear, Little Bear

The cubs were no more than six weeks old the night Carl brought them home from work. Carl had seen them for several days high in a tree at the logging site near the North Fork. Convinced that Mama Bear was dead, he decided to retrieve them. He had to climb the tree to get them down.

"They must have had strict orders not to leave that tree limb until their mother returned. Staying put is exactly what they had been doing," explained Carl.

A guest had left a baby bottle behind at the Lodge. We filled it with a canned milk recipe similar to one Mom had used for me and the boys when we were babies. For the next several weeks we all took turns feeding the bear cubs.

The pups' pen attached to the dog's cook shack became the bear cubs' home when they got big enough. There was a doghouse in there for them to escape the rain. We served them scraps from the kitchen, in a big red bowl as a daily treat. Their pig-like black, beady eyes rolled from side to side as they gulped down the delicacies from the "big house."

Gwen feeds the bear cubs, first with a bottle and then with solid food. They became part of the family for the entire summer. In the fall they were released up Monument Creek. The bears ran a short distance, stopped briefly to look back, then went on their way.

We put dog collars around their thick necks when they became stronger. The more they were played with, the tamer they became. Long walks down the boardwalk and up the airfield became favorite pastimes for all of us.

Every year Carl planted a row of sunflowers in our garden. His mother always had flowers growing in her garden next to the vegetables. When the bears were turned loose to play they would head straight to the row of flowers. They would try and climb up the huge stalks to get to the bright yellow flowers and pull them over.

We realized we would need to turn them loose in the fall, so we notified Fish and Game to ask how to go about it. Agents came up to the Springs to look at the bears and tag their ears. "They would get kicked out of the nest anyway by mama bear if she were in charge. They will survive the winter." So their release was planned.

Visitors at the Springs one summer were enamored with two black bear cubs that the Wilsons had taken in after the mother abandoned them at the North Fork. Here, Carl watches while Jimmy Gray and his grandfather, Blake, interact with one of the bears.

Grandparents Edith and Frank Heller came to visit us several times during our years at the Springs. Here, Rocky and Terry are twelve and ten years old.

We put them in the back of the swamp buggy and headed up the trail toward the Monument Creek cabin. At Spruce Creek we turned them loose. The bears jumped from the back of the swamp buggy to the ground and off they went. Then they stopped, turned and gave us one last look before they scampered into the woods.

Big Bear and Little Bear were never seen again—we think.

Birch Creek Springs and Harding Lake

We all knew there was another hot springs northeast of us on the South Fork of Birch Creek, about 30 miles away. Carl and Chuck had often talked about it, so one Friday evening after work, Chuck flew in to the Springs in his Cub to pick up Carl, Rocky and Terry and fly them over to a gravel bar where the South Fork joined Birch Creek. He had to transport them in two trips because the Super Cub is only a two-place airplane. Rocky and Terry could have easily squeezed together for one trip, since they were about 11 and 12 years old. No one asked if I would like to go along.

It must have been quite an adventure. I heard all about it later. They found the creek where the geological map placed the spring, deep in a ravine where high hills came to a point at the bottom. The creek ran around very large boulders, some as large and as high as the boys' heads. They mostly had to walk on one of the steep side hills just out of the creek. They found the springs, as it dribbled out of the hill and down to the creek, flowing slowly and steadily like the water from our kitchen faucet.

They were all tired from the hike; it was a hot Saturday afternoon so they lay down near the spring to take a nap. Some time later, Chuck woke up hearing a young Dall ram just a few feet away, licking up the spring water. He woke up the others, and they watched for several minutes. When finished drinking, the ram slowly climbed the hill into the spruce timber.

When it was time to leave, the men tried another way back to the airplane, climbing the hill where the sheep went, clear to the top where ridges came together. Then they selected the ridge that was most likely to lead down to the airplane. Their instincts worked well because Sunday morning they came flying back to the Springs tired but overjoyed with their success.

Chuck told us he needed to fly back to town because Sunday afternoon was the newspaper's annual picnic at Harding Lake. Almost as an afterthought, he asked if I would like to go along. He looked at both me and Carl to check for his approval. Carl shook his head okay and a moment later I was off grabbing a few things.

Harding Lake was about 50 miles from Fairbanks. The road had recently been paved, so it didn't take long in Chuck's shiny 1953 Chevrolet pickup. The activity directors had set up games, food and water sports at the Masonic Lodge's pavilion. I think people were surprised to see that Chuck had brought someone with him. I felt like a grown-up lady, attending a social event with such a handsome man.

We stayed for awhile and then drove back to town. He asked if I wanted to fly back to the Springs that night (it stays light all night in June and July) or stay overnight at his folks' place. I opted to stay so that I could visit with friends the next day, until Chuck got off work. I slept on their couch in the front room.

The flight home the next evening was pleasant but as soon as Chuck left, my family bombarded me with questions. The trip to the lake was a nice break from the routine of summer life at the Springs.

Back to Fairbanks for High School

In the fall of 1956, my parents and I decided I would go down to Fairbanks to attend Lathrop High School. We had lived away for my junior high years, and I was ready to try life back in town. Part of me missed seeing the friends I had grown up with. As much as I loved them, my little brothers could be a pain. I looked forward to spending time with kids my age.

At the kitchen table we discussed what the next year might look like. My parents said that being apart would be a big adjustment for all of us; was I ready to go? I said yes, though part of me still had doubts. Mom assured me she would write me letters, and the Bachners and Grays would look out for me, too.

That summer I had noticed Carl and Mom treating me more like a young lady than a girl. I had learned so much, living and working alongside such enterprising parents. I didn't question or yet appreciate the courage it took to try new ideas like reviving the Springs. I was glad my parents showed me how to fend for myself and be open to new experiences, always learning. Carl and Mom carried on the Wilson-Heller tradition of working hard and taking on challenges. Growing up in Fairbanks, I had learned traditional skills of a mid-1950s woman, like cooking, cleaning and responsibly caring for my little brothers.

In these last two years, though, my world had gotten much bigger. The boys and I now knew how to hunt, trap, fly fish, mush dogs, serve meals, and live peacefully among wild animals. Though Carl was the head of our family, he and Mom discussed everything as equals. There was no labeling chores as "women's" or "men's" work. Sometimes Carl cooked, Mom and I built and fixed things— whatever was needed. Their marriage was what other adults called non-traditional.

Later I moved around my room more slowly than usual. I packed up my clothes, books, letters, diaries, and the pink shell from Caribou Ranch, remembering how much fun Joanne and I had exploring all the treasures that the former owners had left behind. I reminded myself that soon I'd get to see her without taking a plane or dogsled.

As usual, I had plenty of time to think. I thought about how kids were supposed to go to school, and what it meant to get an education. I thought about turning twelve, riding in the jeep with Mom, turning off the Steese Highway to follow in the D4's tracks. In some ways that was the first day of my nontraditional schooling.

Without meaning to, I had learned about freedom. Waking with my family in the tent on the side of Mt. Ryan, watching camp robbers dance and poke each other over pancake crumbs, catching early morning grayling from the creek and frying them up for dinner (What could taste better than that?), waiting tables for dozens of handsome soldiers...all these new experiences grew me up in ways I felt but couldn't put into words for other people. When we took off for the Springs I didn't just feel excited. I felt relieved to get away from the teasing of my classmates. I had wondered if that part of living like a frontier-woman might be easier than living in town.

The kerosene lantern caught my eye. As the mantle glowed white like a slide projector bulb, the memories followed one after another—the harder scenes, too.

On the way to the Springs, Mom and I had almost died, sliding down the mountain to Frozenfoot Creek. I was so relieved to be alive that I had thrown away the treasure map without even searching for gold.

But we survived that accident and I learned to accept that sometimes life is not fair. Sometimes you get attacked by mosquitoes and get handed the bug dope last. Sometimes you arrive to find a swimming pool full of algae. From walking through abandoned cabins, I had learned that magazines and fine china don't matter nearly so much as people do. I may not have attended junior high in town, but these were lessons I knew I would not soon forget.

Before I knew it, the day came to return to Fairbanks. My parents had rented our old house in town to Mrs. Gillanders, who agreed to board me for my first year at Lathrop. My brothers helped unload my luggage, then my family drove away toward Phillips Field for their flight back to the Springs. Suddenly I felt alone and nervous. How could I feel so protected out in the wilderness and so alone here? I wondered if my mom and dad felt like crying, too, even though they were Wilsons.

As far as housing, the first year living with Mrs. Gillanders went smoothly, but during my sophomore year I roomed with a lady who my parents paid to board me. I agreed I would take the bus to school. That worked well for two weeks. Then one morning I overslept my alarm and missed the school bus. I asked my host-mom to drive me to school.

"I don't have time to drive you," she said. "I have to get to work."

I felt the old nervous-tummy feeling from when I needed to pour coffee for the Lodge's first dinner guests without Mom in the room. I was not ready for this. "What am I supposed to do?" I squeaked. My heart was racing.

"Well, you'll need to call someone," she said, handing me the phone receiver. She acted like it was obvious I would know how to use the receiver.

I wrapped the twisty cord around my finger. "I don't know anyone except Joanne. And I don't know anyone's phone number by heart." I had hardly ever used the two-way radio at the Springs except for emergencies. "Please. I don't know what to do," I said, trying not to sound desperate.

"You'll need to find someone else or you'll have to walk," she said firmly.

I could feel my face getting hot. "Fine, I'll walk," I answered, feeling all kinds of emotions at once. I turned on my heel and walked down the driveway without looking back even once. "I don't need you or your stupid car," I muttered.

I started walking in the direction of town, but couldn't remember the way to the high school. I was twelve when I last lived in town, so I hardly thought about that kind of thing. I didn't want to look like I didn't know where I was going, so I just kept marching, the way Carl did when he figured out the missing piece of some puzzling project he was working on. I hoped I looked as determined on the outside as I felt inside, but I also felt self-conscious of my limp and of the fact that I was walking by myself. Another wave of fear washed over me.

Three different cars pulled over to the side of the road to ask if I was okay and wanted a ride. Each time I felt nervous who was pulling up to me. Each time I said I was fine, thank you, and kept walking. I knew better than to get into a car with a stranger, even if it was cold out and my body was sore. Soaking in the mineral springs and doing daily exercises had eased the stiffness from my crooked spine and cockeyed hips, but that habit didn't change the length of my legs, so I was out of luck. Walking very far hurt.

Then came the fourth driver. I recognized the lady as a friend of my parents from when I was little. She said she'd be glad to take me wherever I wanted to go. "To Ann Bachner's house, please?" I wasn't surprised that she knew their family, too. Minutes later I rang Joanne's doorbell and her mom Ann opened it, looking shocked to see me on her doorstep. I must've been quite a sight.

Gus Lohi was a solitary full time resident at Munson Creek on the Middle Fork. Gus and Carl became good friends over the years even though they lived 15 miles apart. Gus built this bridge over Munson Creek so he could trap much of the Middle Fork with his dog team.

"Gwen! What happened?" she gasped, her arms wide for a hug.

I explained how I'd missed the bus and had to walk to Lathrop High School.

"She expected you to walk?" Mrs. Bachner asked as we walked toward the kitchen. She pulled a coffee mug off the cup rack. "How about some hot cocoa?"

"Yes, please. The lady said she needed to get to work," I said, trying to sound grown-up and reasonable, but I was furious. What she said was the law.

I looked back at her worried eyebrows. I had never seen Mrs. Bachner so riled up. I was afraid she might burn herself in that state. "Good Lord," she finally exclaimed. "What is that woman's name?"

I got flustered. "I can't remember. I'm sorry, I'm so late for class."

I gulped down the creamy cocoa and we both calmed down, then she looked me straight in the eye. "Gwen, you will stay here tonight. We'll pick up your things after school, but I will not have you going back to stay with that woman." So I didn't. Instead, I got to board at my best friend's house for several weeks, till we found a better living situation. The Bachners treated me like family, and never charged my dad one dime.

With Mrs. Bachner on my side I didn't even get in trouble for arriving late to school. What a relief to feel at home while away from the rest of my family. I thought home and family always went together.

Fish Out of Water

High school was hard. The classes were the easy part, since the Calvert courses had been so thorough and I liked to study. The people were the problem. In elementary school some kids called me "Skinny Gwennie," and at 14 I was still very slim, but I hardly heard that anymore. Now they took to calling me a "hick from the sticks." I was sad to find that even my childhood friends, except for Joanne, turned their noses up when they saw me, like I didn't matter anymore. In those two junior high years my friends had become enemies without my saying a word.

In time I made a new set of friends, including another Gwen like me, but black, whose father was stationed at Fort Wainwright. One day when she was eating lunch alone I asked if I could join her. She said yes, and after that, we ate together almost every day. Other students gave her a hard time for being black, but she never bothered anyone. We became close friends.

For after-school activities, I resumed piano lessons and joined the Lathrop junior dog mushing team. I was pretty good, too. A friend of our family lent me their team of Siberian huskies for racing.

One time my lead dog got spooked by a branch snapping and bolted sideways, knocking me off and into a snow berm. There I sat on my behind, whistling for them to return. Through my parka hood's edging of wolf ruff, I squinted, watching my dogs speed over the finish line without me. I wasn't sure whether to celebrate or cry. Technically speaking, I won, since my sled crossed the line ahead of everyone else's, but the judges didn't see it that way. The boys on the team, which was most of the team, talked about me where I could hear them. "See? I told you a girl can't mush dogs!" I told myself they probably didn't know better. I figured not one of them had a mother who could drive a jeep and trailer backwards down a cliff without jackknifing.

Each summer of my high school years I returned home to the Springs, where I helped Mom and Carl with whatever they needed. They appointed me supervisor of the resort greenhouse. The warm mineral water that Carl pumped into the greenhouse made the vegetables huge and full of flavor. I proudly grew our first tomatoes and cucumbers, which got gobbled up in record time.

Other times I helped serve guests, cook, or tend the animals, which was always my favorite job. I have always loved how each species of animal has habits and patterns that work with the rest of nature. Caribou migration, the return of Lucy the moose, the flight of birds all followed a mysterious rhythm, like they were listening to some grand orchestra, some kind of theme music we humans couldn't hear. They followed their instincts to come and go, to mate and tend their young, to fight or hide, and to retreat when they sensed their time on earth, their melody, was about to end. After so many hours observing nature, I had concluded that animals were much more sensible than people.

I had grown to love living at the rustic resort. I felt tougher. The same weather conditions were more challenging for us in our remote location than when we lived in Fairbanks. In town, neighbors would rely on each other in extreme weather, but at the Hot Springs, we were on our own much of the time. Groceries and medical attention were only a 30-minute flight away, but sometimes minutes counted.

During my senior year at Lathrop, Rocky was a sophomore and Terry, a freshman. We all roomed at the home of Tommy Roberts who had lots of sisters, who Rocky and Terry appreciated. The Roberts were pros at housing lots of kids. During high school the boys skated on the town team. Rocky trapped beaver one winter up the Chena at Flat Creek, which was as far as the town road went. I felt bad for Terry who also got teased at school. He felt homesick so often that I waited for him after school, so we could talk, sometimes through tears, on our walk to the Roberts' house.

The boys continued to help out at the Springs before going their own ways. After graduating from Lathrop, Rocky went back to help Carl build cabins, then went to the university, taking ROTC and business courses. After Terry graduated high school, both boys joined the Operators Union 302 so they could work Cats on the road-clearing contract Carl landed. That project lasted three years.

Trip to Clums Fork

In 1958 Carl promised us a camping trip before we went back to Fairbanks for school. Soon after we turned the calendar to the month of August it began raining. For days we waited for the rain to stop. A week before Labor Day the sun appeared so we left late one afternoon.

Mom stayed at the Lodge to keep her eyes on things.

The weather was crisp when we spent the night at our Monument Creek cabin at the base of Far Mountain. Rocky drove the D4 Cat and Carl followed with the Weasel. He would use the D4 to improve the trail above our cabin and around the base of Far Mountain. After a supper of steaks fried in the big dutch oven on top of the Yukon stove, we spent a pleasant night at the cabin.

In the morning we packed up and continued. The sun was bright and the hillsides were brilliant with fall colors. At the top of the first ridge we stopped so Carl could work on the trail ahead. From there the traveling became more difficult with huge rocks and holes. We parked again and the D4 continued around Far Mountain.

Carl occasionally took hunters out for caribou, bear and moose. He is pictured here with Glen Roberts from California, a friend of both Carl and Chuck. Glen penned a message on the picture: "Here's hoping all your hunts are as good as this one."

After crossing Porcupine Creek we had lunch. We found small deposits of coal, small, unusually beautiful wildflowers and passed by a small herd of caribou feeding on a ridge leading up to Far Mountain. Clums Fork is a creek on the far side of the mountain feeding into Birch Creek.

Carl had been to Clums Fork only one other time on a hunting trip. As we descended the last ridge before dropping into Clums, Carl pointed out the wreckage of an airplane. He told us it was a Grumman Widgeon twin engine airplane piloted by Ernest Patty, Jr., a former WWII Air Force squadron navigator, flying in bad weather from Woodchopper to Fairbanks in the winter of 1947. Tragically, both pilot and passenger were killed in the accident. Six years later, Ernest Patty, Sr., would serve as a visionary and well-loved president of the University of Alaska, Fairbanks.

From there we followed the creek for quite some distance, then proceeded across a thick, timbered flat where strange-looking birds flew up from the underbrush. Soon we came upon the mining shafts that long ago had been dug into the sides of the hills. As we got into heavier timber a few cabins began to appear.

The cabins had been deserted for many years. One was in good condition, nestled in the alcove of a valley, probably protected from harsh weather by the surrounding spruce trees. The cabin looked as if someone had just left for a few hours intending to return soon. Bears and wolverines had gotten in and stirred up the contents as they always do, while squirrels and mice had found shelters and made nests. Oddly, everything the owners had possessed in this wilderness haven was still there.

Some clothing hung on rows of nails across one wall. Dishes and cooking utensils lay on the shelves, or behind the large wood stove. Cans and boxes of food staples were everywhere, a few untouched, others ripped open and the contents scattered about the floor. There were books and magazines dating to the years fur trapping supplemented a prospector's income. We found an old Sears catalog and diaries which charted the owners' daily existence, mentioning trips to the Big Chena Hot Springs for visits, baths and reunions with friends.

Dog meal was still in cans by the door, and from the evidence behind the cabin they must have had many dogs. Some doghouses were still in good condition and others were now rotted by time.

There was evidence of a woman having been there. Faded ruffled curtains framed two of the windows. There were knitting needles, old yarn, an old stained doily on a small dirty table, along with hairpins in a little tin box on a shelf above the washbowl and pitcher. A kerosene glass lamp that had escaped the bears' wrath still had fuel, its wicks ready to ignite, though years of dust covered the unbroken mantle.

"How did they get all this stuff in here?" I asked.

"By horses, probably, or dogsled. Every time they made a trip to town, they hauled more in," Carl said.

I rummaged through all the forgotten articles. We salvaged some of the things from the past and displayed them in the Lodge along with other antiques we had accumulated during our time at the Springs.

A Mother's Love

Chena Hot Springs, Alaska
November 1, 1958
Dear Gwen,

I'm writing this note to you in hopes that the mail plane will make it in tomorrow. No school today, I'm going to wash clothes, and do the usual puttering for a Sunday afternoon.

Now about the formal––I don't know when your Junior Prom is, but I thought it may be before Thanksgiving. So in case you have an invitation and wanted to go I thought you would like a formal dress. (Those dances are formal, are they not?) Gwen, get a nice one, but a moderately priced one. I have no idea what the prices are now-

a-days. Shop around a little. Ask Mrs. Garrett (our host family on Lathrop Street) to go with you and help you on the price––she will know. Of course, Gwennie, I would love to be the one to go with you, but that is impossible, as you know.

We haven't been doing much or anything exciting, just eating, reading and mushing the dogs some. Carl hasn't gone mushing much because he and Frank are hauling logs for our house. Terry goes on Saturday and Sunday with them when we don't have school.

The pups are growing fast and are full of the devil. How is school coming along? Good, bad, or what? By the way has your new girl friend from Fort Wainwright been around anymore?

As you have guessed by this time, Chuck will bring you and Rock home for Thanksgiving. He is invited to stay. You may have to miss a day of school. The days are getting pretty short now.

Love, Mother
P.S. Take this note to Quality Meat and get a turkey for Thanksgiving. Bring it with you when you come up.

Hosting Fairbanks Dog Mushers

For several years Carl invited the dog mushers of Fairbanks to spend a few days at Chena Hot Springs Lodge. In 1959, the invitation was for Easter weekend and I flew up to the Springs to help Mom in the kitchen. Two groups, totaling 20 people and 120 dogs, came up the trail, the first group on Wednesday, and the second bunch on Thursday. It took them about six hours to reach the Lodge from where they hitched their teams into harnesses at the end of the existing road from town.

The weather was rather chilly coming to the Springs, with the thermometer well below zero. There were some glacier ice areas which made it rough for the teams as the dogs do not like to travel over ice. It was a defined trail. Carl had opened our end of the trail when he did some earlier freighting of supplies.

On the return trip Sunday, the temperatures were milder but still below freezing; it was easier for the dogs. The mushers brought a load of dried fish to feed their teams while here at the Springs.

During the two-day stay at the Lodge, the mushers occupied part of their time with such useful tasks as harness mending. Another day was spent mushing to our cabin near Far Mountain, about 14 miles roundtrip. But it wasn't all work. Going for a swim in the pool in the middle of winter was a relaxing treat. The enclosed pool was encrusted with ice on the outside, steamy inside. The thermometer read zero as they scurried along the path through the snow in their bathing suits for a dip in the warm mineral waters.

The cabins glowed with cozy warmth, while the snow-covered hills behind were silhouetted by a display of the aurora borealis. The Lodge is situated at an elevation of 1,200 feet while nearby mountains rise to a height of 3,000 feet and Far Mountain to 4,500 feet. Guests stayed in the Lodge and the cabins. We served the mushers their meals family style, with favorites like moose soup and moose stew. Carl took home movies of the departing sleds to show them next year, when he expected to invite them back again.

In 1959 the mushers attending included John Greenway, Libby Wescott, Jim Lundgren, Cliff Tweedy, Betty Lester, Mrs. V.D. Marsh, Jere Parker, Jo Ann and Donald Peck (the actor Gregory Peck's brother), Ann Weston, Janice Lundgren, Mrs. Grace Hughes, Maj. T. C. Hughes, Johnny Lundgren, Fred Weideman, Bobby Stroecker, Jeff Studdert, Godfrey Joseph, Leslie Patterson, Merle Marie, Herbert Triplett and the photographer from the *Fairbanks Daily News-Miner*, Phil Hoon.

CHAPTER 21

The Bear

Hefty paws and rolls of fat jiggled beneath a thick, black coat of hair as the bear lumbered along the outside of the Lodge toward the back door. We stifled our breaths and watched from the dining room window. The bear's heavy breathing was creepy. The boys and I were right behind Carl and Mom as we all tiptoed into the kitchen and crowded around the small window above the sink. The bear hesitated at the corner logs where the kitchen joined the back room.

Unlike his clumsy footwork, the bear raised his head with princely grace above his shoulders, inhaling the air around him, then swinging his head from side to side.

"Must smell food," Carl whispered.

The bear dropped his head and cautiously stepped onto the wooden stoop beneath the back door. He eyed the screen, pushing on the mesh with a black paw. His nose made another circle through the wind, and his fluffy coat shimmered in the rays of the late evening sun. Then he turned and lumbered around the corner and out of sight as he made his way around the building.

I darted past the food cooler between the kitchen and the back room to the rear window in the back of the storeroom. The bear was already at the window. I leaned into the open screened window to get a better look just as Carl stepped up behind me.

"Hey, Blackie!" Carl yelled at the bear. "What do you think you're doing? Go on home!"

The bear swung his head around and looked up at the window to five pairs of eyes staring back at him. His right paw whacked the log wall beneath the window. I leaped backwards.

"Can't take a joke!" Carl called, grinning as the bear regained his balance.

The bear changed his mind about investigating further. He ambled away, in between the first and second cabins, crossed the clearing and entered the woods on the other side of Spring Creek.

Several days later, without warning, Carl passed out from pains in his lower back. He and the boys had been working all day at the logging site at the North Fork. The boys drove him home. Carl was sprawled out on the bed of the six-by-six International truck. Carl's pains worsened over the next few days until even he could not hold up any longer. The suffering was severe. Carl called for a plane and he and Mom made a trip into Fairbanks to see the doctor. The day he and Mom returned from Fairbanks, just as the plane lifted from the runway to return to town, Carl doubled over again with another attack. The doctor had given him medicine and a special diet, and said Carl would be fine in time. It was his kidneys.

Carl lay on the couch rolling from side to side, his hand pressed firmly against his back above the belt line.

"I know he just saw the doctor, Mom," I argued, "but I think we should call for another plane."

"No!" she said, wiping back tears. "I don't think your dad would want me to do that. He wouldn't like it, not after just having been in town. You know how your father is."

Carl's eyes were closed, his face drained of color. He was stubbornly tough and never allowed anything to get the best of him. But this time I feared the pain was even more than he could stand. I put my arms around Mom and held her as she wept. My anger mounted as I watched the two people I loved most in the world in so much pain.

"He'll be okay, Mom. Go wash your face. You know Daddy wouldn't want to see you like this," I told her. Mom nodded her head and walked to the ladies' room.

To go against Carl's wishes frightened me. To go against Carl's *and* Mom's wishes was something I had never had to consider, much less do. Even so, I knew what had to be done. Carl could get mad if he wanted. I hurried into the dining room. It took several minutes before I was able to get ahold of Wien Alaska Airlines on the two-way radio. I explained the situation and asked them if they would contact Hawley Evans to send a plane back immediately for Carl.

I could only remember one other time Carl had been that sick. We were still living in town then and for some reason the boys and I escaped the effects of a poisonous can of salmon from the night before. Mom took ill first, at home. Carl was running the late show that evening when he took sick and an ambulance was called for him. He said he didn't need a ride, so he left the Empress Theater on foot. He proceeded to stroll past the waiting ambulance as if it had been called for someone else, then walked two more blocks to the river, across the Chena Bridge, and into St. Joseph's Hospital like there wasn't a thing wrong with him.

Mom sighed when I told her what I'd done, but agreed that I had made a good, though tough, decision. Again, she left me in charge of the boys and running the resort. I was 18 and the boys, 16 and 15. I was glad Mom trusted me to keep things running smoothly.

The next morning Rocky and Terry awoke without their usual grumpiness. I knew they must have big plans. They wasted little time in getting to the breakfast table, gobbling down in record time the pancakes I had stacked on their plates.

"Where are you guys going in such a big hurry?" I asked, feeling like the adult in the room.

"Down logging. We're going to get all that cut timber limbed and stacked before Carl gets back," said Rocky proudly. He picked up his empty plate and headed for the kitchen. Terry rose, chewing a last bite of food, and followed Rocky.

"Did he say you could?" I asked.

"Yeah."

Two days later, Blackie paid another visit. I called him Blackie in case he was the same bear we had all watched a few weeks earlier, poking around outside the kitchen window. That time our whole family was together, with Mom and Carl in charge. This was different. The boys were down at the North Fork working. Blackie tried to use the corner logs outside the boys' bedroom as a ladder to get onto the roof. He reminded me of the funny bears I'd seen at the zoo in Seattle when we visited Grandma and Grandpa Heller the summer I was nine. I laughed as I told the boys over supper that night about Blackie's performance and how I chased him away by yelling at him.

The boys returned to the logging site again the next day. I finished up the breakfast dishes, put them away and mixed up a batch of bread. As I kneaded the dough, thoughts of Carl tugged at me. The "not knowing" invited my mind to create a steady stream of the very worst possible outcomes. I certainly didn't want Carl to be ill, but I enjoyed being in charge. The new independence I was feeling and the responsibility I had been given in taking care of the place would not be easy to surrender.

The oven burned all morning. I made a pan of gingerbread and set it to cool on the counter next to four loaves of bread. The aroma was strong. When the kitchen got hot, I opened the windows. I also opened the front and back doors to create a draft through the dining room and the kitchen. I made a tomato and cucumber sandwich with lots of mayonnaise and lettuce, tucked the book I was halfway into under my arm, and went outside to sit on the front step to eat my lunch. I was thoroughly engrossed in my book about a heroine's narrow escape when I heard a loud crash from inside the Lodge, jolting me back to reality. There was another crash, followed by the clatter of metal, maybe tin.

There hadn't been an airplane since Mom and Carl left for town. My first thought was Rocky and Terry had returned from the North Fork. I quickly discarded the idea because I would have heard the truck. They could have had trouble with the truck and walked home.

Chapter 21: The Bear

It might have been only the wind but, still, I was afraid to go into the Lodge, so I walked around to side of the Lodge and peeked through a window.

The dimness inside the Lodge made it very difficult to see. I cupped my hands around my eyes to cut down the glare and leaned forward until my nose touched the windowpane. As my eyes began to adjust I got a view of a large, dark form proceeding slowly for the hallway leading to the bedrooms.

My heart jerked, fluttered in syncopated rhythms, and my stomach tightened into a knot. My body stiffened as the "could bes" danced in my head. *No, not a dog.* I would have known. Totem had recently died, and we had not gotten another family pet. Frosty, our lead sled dog, would have barked like crazy if another dog from the team had gotten loose. Had somebody walked up the trail—somebody other than my brothers?

The image forming before my eyes had nothing to do with any of those things. Standing firm, his neck stretched outward and his entire body swaying from side to side as he inhaled the air around him, Blackie swung his head towards the window like a giant crane moving a heavy load. I stepped away from the window.

"Oh dear," I said out loud. "Blackie's in the Lodge."

He must have gotten in the back door. I have to get him out, but how? A gun...I'd better get a gun.

I ran toward the garage. I flew across the footbridge over the hot water run-off stream, down the boardwalk, past the greenhouse, the cookhouse, and through the gate, into the garage.

Upstairs, the guns are upstairs, I remembered. I scrambled up the narrow stairway towards the catwalk above the garage and frantically searched the shelves where Carl kept his gun collection, cleaning supplies, boxes of bullets, pistol, fishing gear, rifles....

"Oh, which one....This one?" I muttered, grabbing a rifle from the wall, then checking the chamber to see if it was loaded, just the way Carl had taught me. "Oh, good, it's full of ammo."

My heart was pounding. I ran from the garage, out through the gate, back by the cookhouse, the greenhouse, over the bridge and as I approached the Lodge, I wondered what I should do first.

I looked through the window again. Blackie was nowhere to be seen.

"Where is he?" I ran to the dining room window.

There he was in the hall. My throat closed up. The bear's nose was pointed in the direction of the kitchen and I thought I might cry. *Think. Think! Maybe he'll go out the back door.* I felt a sense of relief settle over me with that thought and the urge to cry passed. I decided to enter the Lodge through the front door.

With the gun pointing straight ahead I searched the room, then crept through the doorway and into the Lodge. I could see to the kitchen door, but now there was no sign of the bear. He could have changed his mind and not gone in the kitchen. *Maybe he's in one of the bedrooms.* I made it to the entrance of the dining room and took a quick look down the hallway to the bedrooms. The silence was haunting. I didn't want to go any further. Trembling, I forced my right foot onto the linoleum of the dining room floor. What if he was back in the corner where I couldn't see him? I took another step. Still I did not see the bear.

I heard a grunt from the kitchen. I cautiously took two more steps toward the doorway of the kitchen. I could hear him breathing, shuffling, gasping, and bumping into the counter, rattling the dishes I had stacked so neatly. I moved inside the doorway, the rifle in position with my finger on the trigger. I inched my body around the corner of the kitchen cabinet, my cheek pressed hard against the smooth wooden stock of the gun. There he stood, his back to me, front paws on the countertop, gobbling down my gingerbread.

I lowered the gun and grabbed salt and pepper shakers with my left hand from the shelves by the door and flung them at the bear's backside. Still clutching the gun in my right hand, and my finger on the trigger, I yelled at him.

"You get out of here! Leave my gingerbread alone!"

The bear turned, took one look at me and leaped onto the counter. Gingerbread flew everywhere. With my left hand I grabbed the broom from the corner near the door and swung the broom, with the gun tucked up under my right armpit, still aimed directly at him. I must've looked like a wild woman. I swung again and the bear galloped along the counter, across the army range and jumped to the kitchen sink, leaving a trail of urine all the way.

I yelled and called him names, many of which weren't ladylike and would have gotten me severe consequences if anyone other than Blackie had heard them. From the kitchen sink he jumped to the floor and scurried into the back room and out the open doorway, with me in hot pursuit.

A few yards from the back porch, Blackie suddenly stopped. He calmly turned around and faced me. His eyes like clear dark marbles stared wildly at me. I knew then he wasn't scared anymore, either. I raised the gun, closed my left eye and took aim. The bear lunged at me and I squeezed the trigger of Carl's .300 Magnum, just the way he had taught me.

Blackie's life escaped from within him in low, pitiful yelps. I watched him wobble in slow motion toward the stand of trees and slump into the tall grass. I lowered the gun. I felt guilt slowly encompass my whole being and I fought back tears.

Wilsons are strong. Wilsons don't cry. My legs began to shake and the shaking traveled into my stomach, out along my arms and into my hands. The gun became a heavy slippery piece of wood and steel I could not release, and I began to cry.

I had a firm grip on the gun as I moved carefully to where Blackie lay still, on the grass. I knew better than to assume he was totally dead. He was a big ball of beautiful black fur, except for an area on his neck, which was slowly turning a deep, wet red. *In the neck! Pretty good shot, I'd say.* Even as I was proud of my aim, tears began sliding down my cheeks as the weight of taking a life hit me. I wiped the tears away to see what I had done.

"I'm sorry, Blackie. I thought you were going to come back after me," I whispered to his massive body. "I didn't want to shoot you."

I turned and walked back inside the kitchen and leaned the gun against the wall, and let the tears flow. Baking pans littered the floor. My gingerbread had been reduced to dark brown streaks of smashed dough, thinly spread from one end of the countertop to the other. Bread loaves lay everywhere. The kitchen no longer smelled of cooling gingerbread, but of fresh bear pee. The kitchen was a disaster. I turned my back on the mess to check the rest of the Lodge.

In my bedroom Blackie had left a long, deep gouge across the top of the dresser, scattering my collection of treasures, including the pink seashell I had kept from Caribou Ranch, but it was still in one piece. Blackie must have made this mark of aggression in self-defense, clawing the dresser when he saw the "other bear" staring at him from the mirror. I took a few deep breaths, washed my face, and got to work bringing the place back into order, which helped my heart and stomach to calm down.

By the time Rocky and Terry returned from logging that evening, dinner was ready, another pan of gingerbread sat cooling on a disinfected countertop and I was beginning to laugh about what had happened that afternoon. When I related the story to the boys their reaction was not what I expected.

"Ah, you did not," Rocky said, cocking his head to one side and eyeing me sideways.

"I did, Rocky. He's laying over in the weeds by the meat shack."

"Whadya shoot him with?" Terry prodded.

"Carl's .300 Magnum. It was the only one loaded."

The boys exchanged looks then jumped up and headed for the meat shack. They covered Blackie with tree branches so he couldn't be seen from the air. Bear season was closed.

When Mom returned with Carl, he looked much better. He was never again bothered with back pains and over the next few years, Carl told the story of Blackie's visit. "Don't mess with Gwen's gingerbread. You'll end up in the dog's food."

CHAPTER 22

Moving On

At UAF, the Mining School

I felt like a fish out of water at Lathrop High School, and college gave me many more chances to feel like an alien. The town had changed so much since we left. The University of Alaska, Fairbanks, was originally a mining school, and all men. When the university became co-ed, the guys had a hissy fit, like they were Supermen because they were there first. I didn't see anything special about them, and told them so. I was not about to act like their Lois Lane. This breed of men was so arrogant. If a girl turned them down for a date or would not kiss them goodnight they got mad as though she owed them. I will not mention how I know this.

I practiced the piano long hours, till I heard the janitor's keys as he came to lock up the music building for the night. I walked from the practice room to my dormitory but often could not easily get into the building. There in the glassed-in porch between the two sets of double doors (that opened in sequence, to keep the heat from rushing all the way out every time the doors opened), were

In 1960, Gwen graduated from Lathrop High School in Fairbanks.

those God's-gift-to-women fellows, making out with their girlfriends. More than once I stood beside them waiting, saying "Ahem!" louder and louder till the lovey-dovey couple moved over and let me go up to my dorm room in peace.

I didn't date during those two years at UAF, because I was fed up with the men's attitudes. For fun, I studied, played piano, and wrote. I've always loved writing—journalling, essays— and researching. I started writing of my experiences at Chena Hot Springs. While visiting the Springs in summer, I would write at the kitchen table. Carl would walk by and read some of my scrawled notes, and nod. He never com-mented or critiqued my work. I always wondered what he was thinking. When I learned that Thomas Swan had faith-

In 1964, Gwen graduated from the Oklahoma College for Women.

fully taken notes on their 1905 expedition to find the Hot Springs I felt proud of him, that he was a fellow writer as well as frontiersman. Now there's a real man, I thought.

My second year at the university I moved off campus to a small apartment downtown. Carl gave me a cute red car with a white interior, to putter around town, back and forth to class. Most of the year I could walk the few blocks from my apartment to my new job as a copywriter for the *Fairbanks Daily News-Miner*. Though I never heard the details, I figured Chuck had put in a good word for me with Bill Snedden, the publisher. They

Gwen wed Dennis Eilers in a wedding picture at Chena Hot Springs on October 1968 after Dennis returned from Vietnam.

offered me the writing position and I worked there for the rest of my time in Fairbanks. With my earnings I paid the rent and groceries.

In 1962 I transferred from UAF to the Oklahoma College for Women, and did I ever love it—no boys to deal with. I could focus on learning about music and earning my degree. There I met some women who would end up lifelong friends. One of them introduced me to my future husband.

∽

Post Office

The year after I left for high school Carl built a cabin of sawed logs for the Sneddens, just up the North Fork above Monument Creek. Bill Snedden was also a friend of Fred Seaton, U.S. Secretary of the Interior during the Eisenhower administration. On one of Seaton's trips to Alaska, Snedden wanted to show him Chena Hot Springs, but there was a problem. Cabinet level officers were not allowed to travel in single engine airplanes.

There weren't many twin engine aircraft in Fairbanks at that time. Hawley Evans at Fairbanks Air Service had had a Cessna "Bamboo Bomber," a World War II trainer, but he got rid of it. Luckily, Dick McIntyre, owner of a sporting goods shop in town, had just purchased one of the new Piper Apaches. He also had been a World War II army pilot and ran an air service along with his shop. Dick was hired to fly Seaton and Snedden to the Springs for a few hours one summer day.

The road hadn't been built yet. They talked about how hard it was to improve the Springs without enough business. As the three men discussed our problems, someone mentioned that if we had a post office it would be so much nicer for our family and the old timers down on the North Fork. Those men included: Jim Stanley, Red Johnson, Smitty, Walter Belling, Shorty Harbell, Terry Johnson, and Frank Wells. Of these resort guests, only Wells lived at the Springs full time, but all agreed that having a mail drop nearby would help their growing village carry out business and family correspondence more easily. We could even get supplies at a reasonable cost because Alaska had low postal rates for bush locations.

Before Seaton left, a plan had been hatched. Make the Springs a postal drop point, like several other places in Alaska. Wien Airlines would serve us on their way to other places farther east. It was then that Wien's installed a radio at the Springs so we could report to them with our weather on mail days. That radio proved a godsend over the years, especial-

Bill Snedden (left) was owner of the Fairbanks newspaper. One time he brought his friend Fred Seaton, Secretary of the Interior (on his right) to visit the Springs. Seaton saw for himself the need for a rural post office, then saw that one was established soon after he returned to Washington, D.C.

ly for emergencies, like Rocky's bellyache. We had a post office drop at the Springs until the road from Fairbanks was built.

The Sawmill

Long ago someone, but probably after George Wilson, installed a sawmill at the Springs, beside the creek. The round blade was big, maybe four feet in diameter. The supporting timbers were all rotted out.

Carl decided it needed to be in a more open area for better access in handling logs. There was a good supply of standing spruce killed by fire in the area. He and his crew moved and installed the mill between the runway and Monument Creek. They powered it by the power takeoff on the D4. Over the next few years this mill sawed thousands, maybe millions, of board feet of lumber and three-sided logs for cabins.

Carl obtained a log-turning lathe from the Independent Mill in Fairbanks. He only used it for one cabin because it was troublesome to operate successfully. Most of his buildings used three-sided logs.

Yes, there were cabins and lots of them. In addition to our recreation cabin at Clums Fork, Carl built a new home for us all, located over warm ground near Spring Creek. Carl also built several small attractive cabins, available in different sizes, for folks from town. The cabins were not on our homestead, but mostly along the North Fork, as far downstream as where the West Fork merges. This source of income helped support the operation of the Springs until the road was built.

Winter Freighting

Improvements to the facilities at the Springs involved finding a way to transport heavy freight and basic necessities. Carl wanted to open the winter trail to haul his own freight. Only Carl would try something as difficult as this!

By 1963, local roads had pushed east from Fairbanks as far as Anders' Cache, mile 21. Carl decided to open the rest of the winter trail, about 40 miles, using the old D4. Clearing the trail involved bulldozing three feet of snow aside and bridging creeks by pushing them full of snow and packing it down. This took several days of hard work. For several years before the road was finally pushed through, Carl sometimes had the help of a hired man. They used a wanigan (shed on runners) to live in and moved along as they worked. Fortunately, the Alaska Road Commission had staged dumps of diesel fuel along the route many years before in anticipation of road surveys and construction. Carl just put some of it to good use ahead of time.

Carl had already purchased a used army 6x6 truck from Bobby Miller's surplus yard. It proved to be just the right tool for the job. Many tons of freight were moved to the Springs each March. One spring Carl was given a bunch of old cast iron heating radiators from the Lathrop apartments after the fire in 1957. The heavy units came in various lengths. Carl installed them in the Lodge and some cabins, piping warm water from the springs through them. It didn't produce enough heat to completely replace wood, but it considerably reduced the amount consumed in the stoves.

CHAPTER 23

The End of an Era

Carl's Death

Carl was an unusual person. He could do just about everything, never afraid to tackle a new challenge. Why else would he have bought the Springs in the first place? Getting the place back in working order was a job that few other people would have attempted. Of course Mom played an important role as our teacher, a resourceful frontier-minded woman and, when she wasn't cleaning linens, baking pies, fixing broken equipment, trapping marten or teaching us kids, she was the gracious face of the Springs to our guests.

Carl was a hard worker. He almost never stopped. There was always something more to do or fix. He developed heart trouble before his time. Once he went outside Alaska seeking help in Portland but they didn't seem to be able to help him much. He had spells where he would have to sit down and rest. The doctors gave him nitroglycerin pills to put under his tongue, and that helped temporarily, but he never gave up. He still worked in the timber and ran the sawmill.

The night of January 25, 1975 was bitter cold. No one other than Mom and Carl was at the Springs. My folks had retired for the night. Sometime during the night a noise woke Mom up. She turned over to wake Carl and he wasn't there. She waited, thinking that he would return shortly. When he didn't, she put on her robe and went to find him.

Carl Wilson always looked stern in pictures but he was a devoted father, capable of overcoming the many challenges of bush living.

She searched through the rooms of our house but there was no sign of him. The dogs housed near Spring Creek were strangely quiet, so she headed for the garage, an extension of the house, but still saw no sign of Carl. She called for him as she opened the outside door and there on the bank of Spring Creek, on his back, lay Carl, only lightly clothed. Apparently he had gone to check on a commotion at the dog kennels.

Mom called his name as she stepped through the snow toward him. Laying a hand on his shoulder, she said his name again and again. She shook him, but no response. She ran back inside the house, put on a winter coat, grabbed her mittens and keys and headed back outside. She grabbed his arms, pulled him off the bank and dragged him to the car in the garage. With adrenalin pumping, she was able to lift him up enough to lay him partly on the back seat, then went around to the other side of the car to drag him the rest of the way in. Then on that cold night she headed for the hospital in Fairbanks, 65 miles away.

On that frigid January night in 1975, we lost Carl, our dad, husband, and best friend. The lifeblood of Chena Hot Springs ebbed away!

∿

The Springs had become much more than a wilderness adventure, an investment or a business. It had become our home for over 20 years. Carl always said that Big Oil would change Alaska and the people, that the Springs would be bought and sold. Developers would come and go, but the mineral waters would flow on forever.

EPILOGUE

Afterwards

After the death of my husband Denny in 2011, my incentive and ambition to finish writing this book and get it published melted away. Besides that, my computer crashed, I lost material and lost interest several times—until I got an unexpected phone call from out of the blue. An old friend of our family called to ask how my book was coming along. I told him I had put it on the shelf years ago, but had recently looked at reconstructing the garbled chapters. I offered to send him one or two to look at. That person happened to be Chuck Gray, a longtime friend of our family and former publisher of the *Fairbanks Daily News-Miner*.

Long story short, as the saying goes, we worked together to make the story flow smoothly, to work in the historical material and bring the book to a close. The close: that was the problem. I didn't have one; how does one write the end of her own life story? I had left the Springs for school, except summers, after two years. Which stories should be included to finish the book? Between us, we jotted down some significant events, and I wrote the final chapters.

It seems only fair now, after getting acquainted with our family, that you know what became of each of us, starting with me, Gwen (Wilson) Eilers. As I said earlier, after finishing high school and two years of college in Fairbanks, I transferred to Oklahoma College for Women. I graduated with a Bachelor of Arts in Music, specializing in piano. While teaching elementary music, I met Dennis Eilers on a blind date, for dinner on April Fools' Day.

Denny (as his friends called him) and his buddy (who was dating a girlfriend of mine) were in training for the Vietnam War. Denny served as a captain in the U.S. Army for two years, as a combat photojournalist, witnessing the horrors of war firsthand. Decades before the internet and convenient global communication, he launched Operation Hometown, a program providing updates on the deployed soldiers for their newspapers back home. When he returned from documenting the violence overseas, he flew right to see me. That fall (1968) we married in the Chena Hot Springs Lodge. We had two sons, Jon and Dave. After five years of military service, Denny continued with his freelance photography and writing, relocating about the lower 48 several times, showing our sons various regions of our country. Denny passed away in 2011 at the age of 70. Since his death I continue to live in our country home in Iowa, with our two sons not far away.

Rocky, a third generation Alaskan, was born in Palmer, then grew up in Fairbanks and Chena Hot Springs where he learned mushing, raising sled dogs, trapping, hunting and rural living. His early schooling was by correspondence studies in the Lodge dining room, with Mother his teacher. He graduated from Lathrop High School in Fairbanks as a boarding student and attended the University of Alaska, Fairbanks where he majored in Business Management.

After graduating with a commission as second lieutenant from the Infantry Officer Basic Course in Georgia, he served a tour of duty in Vietnam with the 45th Military Intelligence Company USATPAC 525 MI Group. Rocky and his ARVN counterpart analyzed POW reports of captured documents and tracked enemy movements and activity in the combat zone.

While in college he met his wife, Sandy Kennedy. They raised two children, Sean and Sara, and have three lovely granddaughters, Kailey, Claire and Scarlett. Rocky continues to enjoy hunting, fishing, trapping and trips to the family cabin in the Chena Hot Springs area.

Rocky cofounded the firm of Wilson & Wilson, CPAs with his wife Sandy and serves as the managing and tax partner. He is a Certified Public Accountant and member of several professional groups. He and Sandy still enjoy working at this profession.

∽

Terry was born March 13, 1945 also in Palmer, Alaska, and raised at Chena Hot Springs. He learned the meaning of hard work at an early age, including outdoor skills that our parents taught all of us kids. Carl allowed my brothers free time to explore on their own. Terry had five years of Calvert schooling at the Springs before boarding with a family in Fairbanks for high school.

Terry joined the army in 1965 and a year later was going home from Fort Campbell on leave. An airline strike at the time forced him to use bus transportation where by chance he met Nancy Gouin who lived in Detroit. They became pen pals.

Terry served as a paratrooper and squad leader with the 173rd ABN BDE, fighting in Vietnam's Iron Triangle. In 1966, while assaulting a North Vietnamese Army bunker, Terry was hit with a white phosphorus round, and severely burned over the majority of his body. Triaged to die of his wounds, he fought to survive and spent the next three years in army hospitals; he would not give up. He and Nancy were engaged in August of 1967 and married in April of 1968. During the ensuing 18 years they had three children, Robbie, Debbie and Christina.

Terry was extremely proud of his army service and contributed much of his remaining lifetime to helping children in the Fairbanks area. Terry was well-respected and set an example of tenacity for others to follow. He was awarded a Purple Heart and Parachutist

Badge with Assault Star. He died July 5, 1986 as a result of his combat wounds and is buried at Arlington National Cemetery. In 2005 the Wilson Battle Command Training Center at Fort Wainwright was dedicated in his memory.

∽

My mother, Edithbelle (Heller) Wilson sold the Springs in 1977, after holding out for three years for a price she thought was fair. Three Fairbanks businesspeople bought it. Mom stayed in Fairbanks for ten years before trying other areas of the country, including Atlanta and Juneau, where she had friends. She finally returned to Fairbanks in 1998, bought a newly-built condo and lived out her remaining years near people she had known for most of her life.

∽

Our friend, Charles "Chuck" Gray, born in 1928, was married in 1962 to a public health nurse serving rural Alaska. They raised three boys in Fairbanks. He retired from the newspaper after 48 years but always found time for hunting, fishing, gardening and flying. He still lives in the family home in Slaterville, a Fairbanks neighborhood beside the Chena River, with a prime view of the Cushman Street Bridge and annual spring break-up celebrations. We seem to have maintained a close connection all these years, probably because there was an attraction for each other—a bond that years could not erase.

∽

Today, Chena Hot Springs is a thriving enterprise. A paved all-weather road welcomes summer and winter tourists, as well as locals to deluxe accommodations, including indoor and outdoor swimming pools and an assortment of activities. Winter Aurora viewing is especially popular with Asian visitors. The Springs generate their own electricity from the hot mineral water through an ingenious geothermal power plant (Alaska's first) which can be viewed by the public. The owners grow much of their produce and herbs in a large hothouse. Only an hour and a half drive up the scenic Chena River Valley lands you at this rustic mineral springs that for over one hundred years has helped visitors soak away their stress and for some, rekindle the hope of new discoveries.